The Sacred Path of Eco-consciousness

The Sacred Path of Eco-consciousness

Healing our Culture of Discontent

Alice Iida

The Sacred Path of Eco-consciousness:
Healing our Culture of Discontent

Copyright: © 2014 Alice Iida

Cover Art "Ayahuasca Eclipse" by Howard G Charing
(*www.shamanism.cc*)

Typeset by *www.wordzworth.com*

ISBN: 978-0-9960517-1-2

First Printing, 2014

All rights reserved. No part of this publication may be reproduced, stored in retrieval system, copied in any form or by any means, electronic, mechanical, photocopying, recording or otherwise transmitted without written permission from the publisher.

Alice Iida Publishing
www.aliceiida.com

THANK YOU

*I want to thank and acknowledge
The Pachamama Alliance for their work
in changing the dream of the modern world.*

*I give infinite gratitude to my family, friends,
and the Amazon rainforest so close to my heart.*

Dear reader, I dedicate this book to you.

CONTENTS

Introduction		i
Chapter 1	The Bridge: Healing our Disconnect	1
Chapter 2	Healing our Money Pathology	17
Chapter 3	Healing the Modern World Trance	33
Chapter 4	Work and Wellness	67
Chapter 5	Love, Gratitude, Forgiveness	79
Chapter 6	Purpose and Wellbeing	89
Chapter 7	Meditation: Healing Medicine for Humanity	107
Chapter 8	Storytelling for Future Generations	115
Chapter 9	The Journey Continues	121
Bibliography		127

It's 3:23 in the morning
and I'm awake
because my great great grandchildren
won't let me sleep
my great great grandchildren
ask me in dreams
what did you do while the planet was plundered?
what did you do when the earth was unraveling?
surely you did something
when the seasons started failing?
as the mammals, reptiles, birds were all dying?
did you fill the streets with protest
when democracy was stolen?
what did you do
once
you
knew?

"Hieroglyphic Stairway"—Drew Dellinger

INTRODUCTION

We've reached an important time in our history. We must now choose whether to let our way of life go unchecked, or make some much needed shifts. We are facing enormous challenges globally. We've reached a critical tipping point where we need to reexamine the relationships we have with each other, and our planet. This begins with a transformation of ourselves on an inner level, because without becoming the change first, there is little hope for a lasting planetary shift.

As we have become materially more abundant, we have also become increasingly prone to an inner emptiness that affects us all. We are more medicated, anxious, and depressed as a population than at any other time in recorded history. In a desperate attempt to fill that inner void, we satiate our needs with a consumption of the world's dwindling resources. Fortunately, more and more people are waking up and rising to the challenge of filling that void by living the most meaningful and purpose-filled lives possible.

What does it mean to live a purpose-filled life? Deep within, each of us has a burning, instinctive desire to search for our soul's true purpose. We may wish to discover that purpose, with a hope that it is meaningful, and in harmony with our environment. What if we knew that living from this level would connect us to the divine essence of our own being? Expecting anything less is what leads to our dependency on external, ephemeral pleasures.

For many of us, however, connecting to our life purpose is difficult and elusive. This sense of disconnect in my own life, is the very energy that initialized this book's manifestation. As I struggled to find meaning in my life, I will never forget the day I first heard the evolutionary poet Drew Dellinger recite his poem *Hieroglyphic Stairway*. His question "What did you do once you knew?" played repeatedly in my head. What would *you* do once you knew the enormity of what we are facing?

Eco-consciousness is a way of life where we are mindful, aware, and connected to the earth on which we live. There is without a doubt, a link between our own physical health and that of the planet. We can live the most healthy and successful lives in the world, but when we butcher the environment, we (along with our offspring) suffer. Adopting a sacred practice of eco-consciousness will not only revitalize us, but also bring healing to the earth.

Anxiety to Freedom

The energy behind this book began back in 2009. I had been struggling on and off with depression and anxiety for over ten years. I sought help through the traditional medical route, and was told that with a cocktail of prescription medication and some talk therapy, my problems would subside. Yet, the medications that were supposed to help me were numbing me and perpetuating the root of what was causing my inner turmoil in the first place. For almost a decade, I had been medicated for dysthymia (mild, chronic depression), insomnia, and anxiety. I went through years of weekly psychotherapy. I wondered if I was making any progress.

The stories I am about to share with you taught me, in hindsight, that I didn't need to be numbed. I needed to break down and break open. I learned that a breakdown is an opportunity to transform your life into something much greater. It's knowing that it sometimes requires facing danger head-on before we can become integrated. We all face those dark nights at one time or another. This is just a part of life. In the midst of our pain, though, it is difficult to remember that the dawn is never far, but that to reach the dawn requires that we first pass through the night. In fact, the night becomes darkest right before the dawn. One of the greatest adventures in life is to go through a breakdown consciously.

When we begin to experience a state of unrest stirred by the hopeless state of our health, our life, and even our world—this is when something begins to awaken within, calling for us to change.

INTRODUCTION

The sacred path of eco-consciousness is a culmination of my own journey from separation to freedom, into the collective consciousness of what's unfolding in our modern world. I discovered that as a humanity, we are suffering from an inner hunger that needs to be nourished. The stories, archetypes, and symbols of yore gave me insights into my own experiences. In the book, *The Living Universe,* Duane Elgin writes, "The archetypes and stories we present to ourselves act as beacons guiding us into the future."[i] He goes on to say that in order to explore the guiding images that draw upon the deepest wisdom that humanity has to offer, we must ask three important questions: *Where are we? Who are we?* and *Where are we going?* We ask these questions in the sacred path, and in doing so we come to honor the process of merging the "old" with "new." We recognize that traditional ecological wisdom contain essential secrets to ensuring the longevity of our planet, and must be merged with the progress of the modern world.

My Story

Like Eckart Tolle once said, "I have little use for the past and rarely think about it."[ii] In much the same way, I've made an effort to share my relevant stories without getting caught up in the stories themselves. Throughout my life, I got by as a highly functional person with a rather dysfunctional view of the world. By the time I was in my mid-twenties, I was accomplished and egotistical, but my superficial goals were also making me increasingly neurotic. I walked around in mixed states of anxiety and stress. The anxiety came from carrying around a certain character, which I had spent my entire life constructing. That character was my armor, and it involved a list of shoulds and shouldn'ts, imposed on me by my conditioning. I had successfully been sucked into a black hole of the modern world.

About six years ago, a friend invited me to travel with him to Peru. Little did I know that this experience would proceed to change my entire life. What I experienced there was so paradigm shattering that I initially had no idea how I would integrate it all into my life. In the past six years since this initial experience, I have never again taken a prescription medication for depression or anxiety. I haven't missed the prescription medications that once ruled my life, and have continued to feel grounded (despite life's normal ups and downs). I came to awaken to a completely changed perspective of myself, and the world. I was blown away by how this experience transformed what so many years of prescription medicines and talk therapy couldn't heal. I became determined to discover what had occurred in my life. From this search emerged a journey of discovery that took me to a place I never imagined.

This jungle connection took me into 2009, where I heard Drew Dellinger pose the great question: "What did you do once you knew?" It was during that time I connected with the guides and mentors who were crucial to my journey. I met Lynne Twist, cofounder of *The Pachamama Alliance*, who spoke of the organization's work in the Ecuadorean Amazon. This was the synchronicity that brought me back to my own first experiences in the rainforest. I never forgot how much the jungle lit up my soul.

The Pachamama Alliance inspired me to return to the rainforest I fell in love with. It led me to start my own non-profit organization. I vowed to live a more mindful and conscious life. In September 2010, I left on a journey for Peru and Ecuador. In Ecuador, I would connect with the organization and have a chance to observe the work it was doing. During my travels, I would visit remote towns and villages in the Andes and go into the jungles of Amazonia. I had never felt more alive in my life. I connected with beautiful families who welcomed me into their homes with open arms. They would say to me, "We don't have very much, but we have much love."

I spent some time with a local family on the Island of Amantani in Lake Titicaca, Peru. The island was about 9.28 km^2 in size, full of hillsides, terraced, mostly worked by hand, and planted with wheat, quinoa, potatoes, and other vegetables. There was one nonfunctioning generator on the island, and because of this, I got to live the cycles of night and day. I felt happier in a place where there was no running water or electricity and healthier consuming the foods

INTRODUCTION

lovingly sourced from the land on which my body slept. This was a special time, reconnecting to the heartbeat of the earth. It became clear to me that the disconnect from our natural world was producing a society of pathologically stressed and discontented citizens. In large part, this is what had *me* in such a state of distress. I became convinced that time in nature can work wonders for anyone under stress. Reconnection is essential in our modern world. I needed to explore this further.

During my travels, I grew close to many families. I was particularly touched by one family I spent time with in the Sacred Valley of Peru. At night, the mother of the family would show me her beautiful alpaca designs and share stories of how she taught the women in her community to weave so they would have a method of making a living. I learned how the family developed an incredible organic farming system on their land and would barter what they grew with others in the community. In fact, some people in these communities had never even handled money. They had always lived off a bartering system—an exchange of services.

Julio Valladolid Rivera, an agronomist from Peru, has said that the campesinos in the Andes have no need to "re-indigenize." They seed their acreage and scattered parcels and are in tune with the natural cycles of nature. He says that the people who leave and get professional training are the ones who need to "re-indigenize." Professional training has them forgetting the process of agrobiodiversity, which is intrinsic in the knowledge of cultivation in the Andean culture. Rivera says that as technicians, maximum production is always a priority. However, the campesinos cultivate with care and dedication. After being a university professor for twenty-two years, he had to immerse himself in the re-indigenization process, learning from these campesinos. Since scientific methodology is of little use to them, he had to learn how to commune with the plants, which is a key knowledge system in arid farming regions that are dependent on rain.[iii]

The Andes region originated one of the oldest (approximately ten thousand years old) forms of agriculture in the world. Sacredness, reciprocity, respect, and nurturing are key concepts embedded in their worldviews. They hold the pillars of dialogue within communities, bringing balance to humans and the natural world. These are the knowledge systems from which we have moved away in the modern world. One of the greatest dangers facing these knowledge systems is our insatiable appetite for development and the exploitation of nature. The second-biggest danger is the disappearance of the languages that revolve around an oral tradition. We may permanently lose their valuable Traditional Ecological Knowledge (TEK). This is the knowledge about traditional tools used for subsistence, agriculture, healing, medicine, midwifery, ethnobotany, celestial navigation, and archaeo-astronomy.

In many cultures, traditional knowledge has been orally passed for generations from person to person. Some forms of traditional knowledge are expressed through stories, legends, folklore, rituals, and songs. Traditional knowledge has been defined as "a cumulative body of knowledge, know-how, practices and representations maintained and developed by peoples with extended histories of interaction with the natural environment. These sophisticated sets of understandings, interpretations and meanings are part and parcel of a cultural complex that encompasses language, naming and classification systems, resource use practices, ritual, spirituality and worldview[iv]." Regardless of origin, what lies at the root of these knowledge systems is the understanding that we are all completely interrelated as a species.

While traveling in Peru, I connected with various communities in the Andes through the *Instituto de Ecología y Plantas Medicinales* (IEPLAM), where I learned about their efforts to preserve their knowledge of medicinal plant traditions by merging it with the modernization of Peru. I met the director of the *Asociación Chuyma de Apoyo Rural* in Puno, who explained how they, too, were working to keep the indigenous traditions alive in their communities. He gifted me with a manual containing thousands of years' worth of their knowledge systems: *Señas y Secretos de Crianza de la Vida* (Signs and Secrets of the Creation of Life). I held in my hands thousands of years' worth of ancient

INTRODUCTION

wisdom on how to thrive in the natural world. The dots were coming together.

Then, while in Puno, something happened.

I connected with an elder in the Aymara region of Chucuito in Peru. She told me stories in her native tongue, Aymara. I learned that she was a highly revered coca leaf reader in her community. The coca leaf (*Erythroxylon coca*) can be considered the sine qua non of all offerings in the Aymara tradition. Today, coca is part of the ritual paraphernalia of every Aymara practitioner. The *yatiri* (community healers) use the coca leaf as a form of divination. The *qolasiri* (community doctors) use it as a medicine and, occasionally, as an anesthetic. The midwife uses it, among other plants, in childbirthing remedies. In this case, the elder was a well-respected *yatiri*. She asked if I wanted my leaves read. I replied that I did. Coca leaf reader Doris Rivera Lenz has described the process of divination with coca as, "Meeting with the spirit of the element that you are working with. In the case of coca, you meet the mother spirit, soul or power of the plant, which is the sacred part which never dies. The practitioner must be in total communication: spirit-to-spirit. It is more like listening to the coca leaves than reading them. It is a higher state of consciousness. You have to be prepared to integrate yourself spiritually to help another spirit."[v]

As the elder threw her coca leaves on her mesa cloth, the first thing she said to me was, "You are going to have a baby within a year." I thought to myself, why isn't she telling me that I'm on the right path and that I should continue doing exactly what I'm doing? That's what I *needed* to hear. Pregnancy was *not* on my radar. There was no space for motherhood to enter my life. I dismissed it and continued on my journey. Life is mysterious and often has other plans for us. I believe that we are always brought what we need most in our lives to push us forward in our evolution.

Suddenly, in the midst of newfound grandiose purpose and activity, the paradigm of my world once again shattered. The elder with whom I had connected in Chucuito had tapped into a universal information system. I could only hypothesize that she had tapped into information available through the spirit of the coca leaf in the stream of conscious creation itself, an information source available to us all. By the end of 2009, I was pregnant, and I had a beautiful baby boy within a year. I was so stunned by the accuracy of her prediction that I decided to take a pause, to stop, to listen. Life was trying to tell me something.

This was the period in my life that allowed me the space to delve deeper into my inner wisdom. Listening means forgetting yourself completely. It allows you to become a receptivity, a womb. It's a full embodiment of the feminine archetype containing the quality of water and the emotions. Motherhood burst forth sensitivity, intuition, and compassion. Indeed, this reconnection led me into the greatest rite of passage of my life. The ancient cosmological wisdom that I had encountered in Amazonia remained the heartbeat of my journey into motherhood. My husband and I brought our son into the world in the quiet comfort of our home. We shared in the most sacred, yet natural process of birthing. What I came to understand on an even deeper level, was that reconnecting to nature also meant tapping into the inner wisdom that lies within. My biggest task while pregnant was to forget everything I had previously read or seen in movies about pregnancy and labor. Because we are surrounded by so many birthing technologies, we have lost faith in our own natural ability to birth. The mystery of birth can't be understood with the mind. We must instead remember our instincts, and birth through our hearts.

Women in our modern world must rediscover the primordial knowing and innate capability that exists within. In a sense, each of us comes into the world with a specific blueprint for thought patterns and assumptions about what we believe it means to be human. The more aware we become of what is in our unconscious and conditioned learning, the better able we come to see things for what they really are. This awareness is the path of eco-consciousness. I came to know it through creating, carrying, and birthing a new life in a way I had never previously known it. Through the path toward motherhood, the woman creates and infuses new life into humanity's collective consciousness.

INTRODUCTION

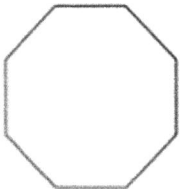

The journey is represented by the symbol of the octagon. The eight sides represent resonance and nurturing governed by the Moon Goddess. Before I could move forward, I was being called upon to embody the four phases of the moon, which represented birth and renewal. Eight multiplied by eight is sixty-four, and there are sixty-four codons in human DNA, sixty-four hexagrams in the I Ching, and sixty-four squares on a chessboard. This is the symbol of nurturing new life. The figure eight itself is a representation of infinity and healing.

In her book *Women Who Run With the Wolves*, Jungian analyst Clarissa Pinkola Estés tells the stories of the female archetypes that represent the different phases in a woman's life. She talks about the woman's body being a storehouse of wisdom, especially the celebration of one of the most important changes in a female's adult life. Motherhood is the discovery of the power of fertility as a direct personal experience, in contrast to the knowledge of it taken from the outside. This is a process of discovering the beauty of the female form through strength. The markings left on the body from pregnancy and childbirth transform into icons of natural female power that have been unleashed in the process. In Taoist teachings, this is called "the gateway." Whether you are male or female, every person on this earth enters the world through the gateway of the woman's womb.[vi]

This was an important part of my journey, without which I would not have been able to complete this book. It taught me to understand that I was always supported by a fertile impetus, one that desires every one of us to create and evolve. With a greater awareness, I saw that the future of our world depends completely on our ability to tap into the vast web of knowledge interwoven in a set of solutions that have been grounded in four billion years of evolutionary intelligence.

The Sacred Path of Eco-consciousness

In *The Living Universe*, Elgin writes about the non-living universe. This is a world where there is no higher purpose or meaning to life. It's a place where love and happiness are simply chemical reactions in the body that have no other significance. In a non-living universe, there is no future beyond our own personal existence. In such a world, material possessions and accomplishments are the prime expression of a person's identity and are thus an important source of happiness. This is the universe in which we humans have the right to exploit the earth for our purposes. Materialism and exploitation are the natural outcomes of such a perspective. We humans have separated ourselves from nature to the greatest extent possible, and if we are to continue to evolve and realize our potential as a species, we must become conscious of our partnership with each other and with nature.

The sacred path of eco-consciousness is about developing a close relationship with the natural world. As we come to alignment, a larger consciousness awakens in each of us. This is the principle of ecopsychology, and on a more fundamental level, the principle of shamanic healing. By strengthening the emotional bonds between people and the natural world, they feel less alienated from nature and more inspired to live a sustainable life. The eco-conscious path involves a firm relationship with our natural world, a practice that allows you to open yourself up to a relationship with the sacred. It is an embracing and mourning of the ecological crisis that is unfolding. This path calls for a commitment to doing the inner work required to feed the soul.

We examine our assumptions with a willingness to transform them, and follow a practice that allows us to re-wire our negative thought patterns. We vow to fully connect to our soul purpose, and converge with others who have the same commitments. This path surpasses our concept of what is even possible in the world. As we connect to our source, and in turn, ourselves, we allow the stories we've created to change from those of separation to connection, from those of fear to hope, and from those of destruction to restoration. At

INTRODUCTION

the base of a mountain in Inferno I, Virgil tells Dante that if he wants to reach the summit of the Mountain of Salvation, he must go down to the very bottom of the earth and begin his climb from there. The only way up is down. A conversion of perspective is needed, such that what appears as up now appears as down. It is only by turning the world upside down or inside out that you can, as Jim Morrison of *The Doors* would have said, "break on through to the other side." And so we begin.

CHAPTER 1

The Bridge: Healing our Disconnect

The symbol you see is known as the *Antahkarana*. This is an ancient healing and meditation symbol that has been used in Tibet and China for thousands of years. It is part of the spiritual anatomy that connects the physical brain and the higher self. It is said that the symbol contains its own consciousness, and being in its presence is enough to change the consciousness of the person looking at it. This can be seen as the bridge to your inner being. It is thought that if you are to ever grow spiritually, you must develop and heal this bridge, this connection.

The Antahkarana is a cube-shaped symbol. It has on its surface three "sevens," which are thought to correspond to the seven chakras, the seven colors, and the seven tones on the musical scale. In the apocryphal book of Revelations, there are the three sevens for the seven trumpets, the seven candlesticks, and the seven seals. Its energy moves through all dimensions, leading us to our higher self.

THE SACRED PATH OF ECO-CONSCIOUSNESS

My first experience in the Peruvian Amazon would alter the course of my life forever. It is the synchronicity that would propel me to return to the jungle repeatedly. Before that experience, I was heavily engrossed in the dream of the modern world. Thomas Berry described this best when he said, "Our entire modern world is itself inspired not by any rational process, but by a distorted dream experience, perhaps by the most powerful dream that has ever taken possession of human imagination. Our sense of progress, our entire technological society, however rational in its functioning, is a pure dream vision in its origins and in its objectives.[vii]"

I was the poster child of the American Psychiatric Association in a society where stress, depression, irritation, premenstrual syndrome, fatigue, and even anger—are all candidates for medication. My psychiatrist had me on Ambien for insomnia, Mirtazapine (an NaSSA) for depression, and Lorazepam (*a benzodiazepine*) for anxiety. For years, I believed I had a psychological ailment, and I never went to bed without some form of pharmaceutical aid; I lived off a haze of artificial sleep. The NaSSA made me gain weight, and the benzodiazepines made me feel numb. Never before had I questioned whether I was suffering from the symptoms of a widespread "culture of discontent" (as anthropologist Meredith Small would call it).

A trip to Peru jolted me out of my trance. My first visit there consisted of a journey into the Amazonian rainforest and participation in a sacred sacrament of which I knew very little. About a week before my departure, I discussed with my psychiatrist a ceremony I was planning to attend in the jungle. At that time, I didn't know what the ceremony would entail—only that I had to be taken off all medication cold turkey. I didn't know then that I would never have to fill another prescription ever again. It took me a while to process what I experienced in Amazonia. I began searching for accounts of other people's experiences. I was intrigued to read Kira Salak's *National Geographic* article, where she shares how the severe depression that had ruled her life since childhood miraculously vanished after visiting the jungle. She wrote, "This was the meat and potatoes of my several years of therapy. Expensive therapy. Who did what, when, why. The constant excavations of memory...And in all that time, after all that therapy, only one thing worked on my depression—an ayahuasca 'cleansing' with Amazonian shamans.[viii]"

Vine of the Soul

I had never previously experimented with the use of psychedelics. I knew that altered states of consciousness were possible through meditation. I didn't know much else about these realms. Many people delve deeply into the pre-work of ayahuasca before their first encounter. I, on the other hand, walked into this situation with very little knowledge of the medicine…and no expectations.

I will never forget the first time I encountered this plant—that feeling of no return. When it finally hit me, I was overcome with the most torturous and gut-wrenching nausea I had ever known, and I entered what I once heard someone describe as a "battle royal with the darkest forces within." I wanted out, but there was no escape. She (the vine) was in my body and circulating through me. Every time the ayahuasquero would begin singing his *icaros* (medicine songs) and rattling his *chakapa* (leaf rattle), it left me squirming painfully, begging for him to stop. The maloca where I lay kept spinning around me uncontrollably. I could smell a stench of ancient remembrance. During the unbearable moments, I would begin counting—*one, two, three, four*—but I barely had the energy to count. I was too weak to shout out. I felt spirits around me, laughing. I imagined I was being mocked. I repeated "This too shall pass," and yet, with no concept of time, a minute felt like an eternity.

I was certain that I was dying. I pleaded with my heart to continue beating. I thanked it for all its hard work. I wanted to vomit but didn't have the stamina. My body was failing me. I was overcome with the most excruciatingly painful realization that I was too fragile to be in this world…too sensitive, too easily bruised. Like a movie, I watched all the flashbacks of my life where I had been hurt by someone, felt judged, watched, and inadequate. I was vulnerable, defensive, and threatened; this sensitivity was the root of so much of my pain, anxiety, and depression. I then felt the unbearable pain of our humanity. We were becoming increasingly separate from our earth—our source—and I could feel the ground on which I lay weeping and pulsating through me as I also began to weep. The superficiality of my life, in my modern world dream, was too painful.

The ayahuasquero came to me and asked that I sit up. I told our sitter that I couldn't move; I was too weak. Finally, with every ounce of strength I could muster, I sat up as Don Ignacio rattled his leaves over my head as he sang his medicinal music. I had seizures of discomfort. I was overcome with a desperate need to purge, and I began vomiting uncontrollably. Here I was, in the Amazonian rainforest, amidst a symphony of life. In that one evening, I felt like I had just released five thousand lifetimes' worth of pain. It was as if I had gone through an exorcism, followed by a feeling of total surrender. I had gone from the certainty that I was experiencing the Divine Comedy—Dante going through the nine circles of suffering located within the earth. From Purgatory to Paradise, I emerged bodiless and formless.

"Ayahuasca," a Quechua word meaning "vine of the soul," is a name given to a brew of Amazonian plants that shamans have boiled down for centuries to use for healing purposes. To the indigenous peoples of the Amazon Basin, it is a medicine that has been used for hundreds, perhaps thousands, of years. One of the two principal plant ingredients of this brew is N,N-dimethyl-tryptamine (DMT), a hallucinogenic that is also secreted naturally in small amounts by the human brain. DMT is classified as a Schedule I/Class A illegal drug in the United States, but in the countries bordering the Amazon Basin, it has been an integral part of their culture.

A number of different plants growing in the Amazon contain the DMT that gives ayahuasca its visionary powers; *Psychotria viridis*, a bush of the *Rubiaceae* family, is most widely used. However, even when DMT is extracted from a plant, monoamine oxidase, an enzyme that occurs naturally in our stomachs, destroys DMT on contact and renders it orally inactive. The other principal ingredient of the plant is the ayahuasca vine itself, the *Banisteriopsis caapi*, which is a member of the *Malpigia* family of forest lianas. It contains chemicals known as monoamine oxidase inhibitors, which switch off the stomach enzyme and allow the DMT to do its work.

Anthropologist Jeremy Narby wrote, "So here are people without electron microscopes who choose, among some 80,000 Amazonian plant species, the leaves of a bush containing a hallucinogenic brain hormone, which they combine with a vine containing substances that inactivate an enzyme of the digestive tract which would otherwise block the hallucinogenic effect. And they do this to modify their consciousness. It's as if they knew about the molecular properties of plants and the art of combining them, and when one asks them how they know these things, they say their knowledge comes directly from hallucinogenic plants.[ix]"

The ingestion of ayahuasca has been associated with a long list of documented cures. In fact, the Peruvian Ministry of Health, aware of the potential in this ancient wisdom, subsidizes an *Institute of Traditional Medicines*. France, who participates in a research through the French Institute of Andean Studies, created a treatment Center for drug addicts in Tarapoto, Peru with their Peruvian counterparts (called *Takiwasi*). The treatment protocol blends traditional medicine and modern psychotherapeutic techniques. It consists of 2 phases: a detoxification using plant purgatives designed to shorten and diminish withdrawal symptoms, followed by a longer second phase of "psychic" detoxification. This second phase includes periodic ingestion of psychotropic plant substances, like ayahuasca[x]. It is said that the patient who undergoes this type of therapeutic process experiences a rebirth of the inner self, manifested through dreams, visions, flashbacks, and symbols. The person is encouraged to eject the toxins that don't belong to him/her, on both the physical and psychological levels, to return to a more integrated sense of the "Self."

Medical Research

In the past couple of decades, a handful of researchers have devoted time to studying ayahuasca. Charles Grob, M.D., a professor of psychiatry and pediatrics at the UCLA (University of California, Los Angeles) School of Medicine, has been at the forefront of this research. In 1993, Dr. Grob launched the Hoasca Project, an in-depth study of the physical and psychological effects of ayahuasca on humans. His team went to Brazil (where the plant mixture can be taken legally) to study members of a native church, the União do Vegetal (UDV), who use ayahuasca as a sacrament. He compared them to a control group that had never ingested the substance. The studies found that all the ayahuasca-using UDV members had experienced remission without recurrence of their addictions, depression, or anxiety disorders. In addition, blood samples revealed a surprising discovery: Ayahuasca appears to give users a greater sensitivity to serotonin (one of the mood-regulating chemicals produced by the body) by increasing the number of serotonin receptors on nerve cells.[xi]

Unlike most common antidepressants (which Grob says can create such high levels of serotonin that cells may actually compensate by losing many of their serotonin receptors), the Hoasca Project showed that ayahuasca *enhances* the body's ability to absorb the serotonin that is naturally there. "Ayahuasca is perhaps a far more sophisticated and effective way to treat depression than SSRIs [antidepressant drugs]," Grob concludes. He insists that ayahuasca has great potential as a long-term solution for the treatment of depression.[xii]

The Multidisciplinary Association for Psychedelic Studies (MAPS) recently completed the first North American observational study of the safety and long-term effectiveness of ayahuasca treatment for drug addiction and dependence in a rural First Nations Community in British Columbia, Canada. The paper documenting the results of the study was published in June 2013 in *Current Drug Abuse Reviews*[xiii]. Findings showed statistically significant ($p < 0.05$) improvements for scales assessing hopefulness, empowerment, and mindfulness suggesting participants may have experienced positive psychological and behavioral changes in response to this therapeutic approach.

I was intrigued by how such intense, positive psychological change took root in me when I was in the Amazon and the mechanics of how such changes went hand in hand with the powerful visions experienced in ceremony, thus playing a role in alleviating my own anxiety and depression. I also wondered if most of what I considered to be anxiety or depression was more a major sense of disconnect from the natural world—a momentary lapse of remembering where I came from—and whether it was the experience of a vastly profound reconnection with nature in the natural space of the Amazon that allowed me to awaken once more.

According to Grob, ayahuasca provokes a profound state of altered consciousness that can lead to temporary "ego disintegration," allowing people to move beyond their defense mechanisms into the depths of their unconscious mind. This unique opportunity, he says, cannot be duplicated by any non-drug therapy methods. "You come back with images, messages, even communications," he explains. "You're learning about yourself, reconceptualizing prior experiences. Having had a profound psycho-spiritual epiphany, you're not the same person you were before."[xiv]

Many ayahuasca researchers agree that the brew appears to affect people on three different levels: the physical, psychological, and spiritual. This complicates efforts to definitively catalogue its effects, let alone explain specific therapeutic benefits. Ralph Metzner, psychologist, ayahuasca researcher, and editor of the book *Sacred Vine of Spirits,* says, "Healing with ayahuasca presumes a completely different understanding of illness and medicine than what we are accustomed to in the West. But even from the point of view of Western medicine and psychotherapy, it is clear that remarkable physical healings and resolutions of psychological difficulties can occur with this medicine."[xv]

Dr. Rick Strassman, author of DMT: The Spirit Molecule, shared his findings on DMT based on scientifically valid data combined with spiritual and religious observations and teachings. The general hypothesis is that the pineal gland produces psychedelic amounts of DMT at certain extraordinary times in our lives. He says, "Pineal DMT production is the physical representation of nonmaterial, or energetic, processes. It provides us with the vehicle to consciously experience the movement of our life force in its most extreme manifestations." He goes on to describe specific examples of this phenomenon, "When our individual life force enters our fetal body, the moment in which we become truly human, it passes through the pineal and triggers the first primordial flood of DMT. Later, at birth, the pineal releases more DMT. In some of us, pineal DMT mediates the pivotal experiences of deep meditation, psychosis, and near-death experiences. As we die, the life force leaves the body through the pineal gland, releasing another flood of this psychedelic spirit molecule.[xvi]"

Dr. Strassman explains that the pineal gland possesses the highest levels of serotonin anywhere in the body (which is a crucial precursor for pineal melatonin). The pineal also has the ability to convert serotonin to tryptamine, which is a critical step in DMT formation. The unique enzymes that convert serotonin, melatonin, or tryptamine into psychedelic compounds occur in high concentrations in the pineal. These enzymes, the *methyltransferases*, attach a methyl group—that is, one carbon and three hydrogens—to other molecules, thus *methylating* them. Methylate tryptamine twice and you have di-methyl-tryptamine (DMT). Because it possesses the high levels of the necessary enzymes and precursors, the pineal gland is the most logical place for DMT formation to occur.[xvii]

Strassman goes on to describe how the pineal gland also makes other potentially mind-altering substances: *beta-carbolines*. These compounds inhibit the breakdown of DMT by the body's monoamine oxidases (MAO). One of the most striking examples of how beta-carbolines work is ayahuasca. Certain plants that contain beta-carbolines are combined with other plants that contain DMT to make this psychedelic Amazonian brew, which allows the DMT to become orally active. If it were not for beta-carbolines, MAO in the gut would rapidly destroy the swallowed DMT, rendering it ineffective. It is uncertain whether beta-carbolines by themselves are psychedelic; however, they do markedly enhance the effects of DMT. Thus, the pineal gland may produce both DMT and chemicals that magnify and prolong its effects.[xviii]

THE BRIDGE: HEALING OUR DISCONNECT

An Interrelated World

When I remember my experiences with the jungle vine, I think of what quantum theorist David Bohm describes as a holographic universe with coexisting realms of reality. The universe is one big hologram that is regenerated at each moment. The entire cosmos is a dynamic projection from a common ground that is holographic in nature. At every moment, each part of the universe contains information about the whole. Bohm views everything in the universe as inseparably interwoven with the life force of the universe.[xix]

It became clear to me that I was a participant in the totality of the universe and that I could instantly transport myself, in defiance of all time and space, into strange realms. The plant led me to examine my own failings and weaknesses in an unsympathetic light. The self-flagellations were inescapable. My ego used all its force to convince me that I was dying, and death was the most terrifying moment of my existence. The more I fought against my ego, the worse my experience was. I felt physically paralyzed and my voice was gone, unable to express what I was feeling. We in our modern world are so used to suppressing what we feel. It is said that until we stop repressing painful feelings, we will never be healed of physical and psychological issues.

At my most terrifying moment, I had a realization that when I surrendered my ego, the terror would transform into a state of peace. I felt the entire fabric of my being dissolve into millions of dust particles, and I thought to myself, *I am dying, and it's beautiful*. As I dissolved, I melted into the mud of our earth and felt myself absorbed through every molecule of dirt. I was traveling deep into the core of our earth. When I realized this deeply profound sense of interconnection with all that is, I suddenly felt myself rise from the earth and emerge as a flower. It was the most life affirming experience I could have ever had. I then found myself underwater and noticed that I was some prehistoric aquatic dinosaur. As I swam, I could feel the density of my ginormous body flowing through the water, and I was surrounded by prehistoric life. I knew in an instant that I was being reminded again that this is where I had come from. I am billions of years old, and we are all one. I was brought down on my knees in humility. I felt deeply grateful for my life and felt a reverence for all life on earth. It was the most beautiful thing I have ever experienced, and if this is anything like what poets describe as heaven, I no longer felt any fear of death. The mystical experiences of oneness that I had always read about in the spiritual teachings of the *Vedas* suddenly became experientially real. *This,* was yoga.

The journey was about abandoning identity and losing faith in material form. I was a blank mirror staring at the screen, observing the formless source begin to dissolve the self. The evolving spirit grows in this state of being: washing away the artificial shell, the beliefs, structures, thought forms, and preconceptions of perception, and returning to the thoughtless, desire-less, unmanifested, and unconcerned awareness of the stream of life. Thought forms become nonexistent, and you no longer see life as a conglomeration of fears and worries. This is the space I discovered—where no opinion on life or experience penetrates the ego whatsoever. I finally understood that in this space, the lotus flower blossoms.

By stripping away the ego and allowing me to return to the "source," ayahuasca helped me remember a place within myself that was long forgotten. The ego of the current human condition often asserts itself as a false self, while our true nature lies hidden. Many of us have forgotten who we are and forgotten the eternal landscape that we inhabit. The journey back to the true self is a natural process that occurs when the sleeping brain awakens. When this happens, our point of reference is moved, and by letting go of who we *think we are*, we begin the journey "home."

Shamanic traditions refer to this as the "death of ego," where ideas of self-importance naturally fall away. If you have watched the movie *Avatar*, you will remember the scene about reconnecting with nature by way of the Na'vi's neural connection through their tails. The Na'vi could link to any other living thing on Pandora through this connection. The Na'vi's nearly telepathic understanding of their environment was grounded in ritual, plant-lore, and an *organic communications network*. This network was represented by the fibrous ponytail tentacles that not only allowed the Na'vi to form direct control links with animals but also (through the optical filaments of the *Tree of Souls*) to commune with both ancestors and the Eywa, the spirit of the planet whose name resonates with *Erda*, or Earth. Much like the Na'vi tail, ayahuasca is also an interface.

Ayahuasquero Ronald Rivera Cachique said, "Ayahuasca subjects us to more intense analysis and the questioning of all our presumptions, upon which we base our existence. Many of our ideas about life may be wrong, and these mistakes in the way we understand life and reality can lead us to errors, creating physical and mental abnormalities or diseases within us. The Ayahuasca trance specifically allows us to put into question all truths so that they can be clarified or reaffirmed with new and richer perspectives of understanding."[xx]

I find it fascinating that there are theories that suggest that Moses was in an altered state of consciousness when he brought the Ten Commandments down from Mount Sinai. Benny Shanon, Professor of Psychology at Jerusalem's Hebrew University, has said that two plants found in the Sinai Desert contained the same psychoactive molecules as those found in the plants from which the powerful Amazonian hallucinogenic brew, ayahuasca, is prepared. "In advanced forms of ayahuasca inebriation, the seeing of light is accompanied by profound religious and spiritual feelings," Shanon wrote. "On such occasions, one often feels that in seeing the light, one is encountering the ground of all Being...many identify this power as God." He said that *harmal*, contained in one of the psychoactive plants found in the Sinai, had long been regarded by Jews in the region as having magical and curative powers.[xxi]

New research also suggests that Paleolithic cave paintings (like those in the Lascaux caves in southwestern France) were created by men in altered states of consciousness influenced by similar hallucinogenic substances. After analyzing the patterns found in thousands of years' worth of prehistoric cave art of vastly different times and places, scientists from Tokyo found similarities between paintings in different areas. According to a study published in the journal *Adaptive Behavior*, these similarities are "best explained by the common experience of these patterns as geometric hallucinations during altered states of consciousness induced by shamanic ritual practices."[xxii]

The Portal

Anthropologist Jeremy Narby, in his book *The Cosmic Serpent*, writes about how research indicates that shamans access an intelligence through ayahuasca, which they say gives them information that has correspondences with molecular biology. His research examines the symbology of ayahuasca, which is often portrayed as a snake. He further explains that in the book *Ayahuasca Visions: The Religious Iconography of a Peruvian Shaman*, the approximately fifty paintings by the ayahuasquero Pablo Amaringo have a striking resemblance to many people's experiences of ayahuasca, including his own. Many of these paintings contain symbols and images of zigzag staircases, entwined vines, twisted snakes, and double helixes.[xxiii]

The Australian aborigines consider the creation of life to be the work of a "rainbow snake" whose powers were symbolized by quartz crystals. The Desana of the Colombian Amazon also view the cosmic anaconda, guided by the divine rock crystal (quartz), as the creator of life. In Joseph Campbell's *Occidental Mythology*, one can find image after image of serpents in most of the sacred scenes. Campbell himself wrote about the snake symbolism, saying, "Throughout the material in the Primitive, Oriental and Occidental volumes of this work, myths and rites of the serpent frequently appear, and in a remarkably consistent symbolic sense. Wherever nature is revered as self-moving, and so inherently divine, the serpent is revered as symbolic of its divine life."[xxiv]

Throughout mythology, one sees the symbol of the serpent repeatedly. In ancient Egyptian drawings, one can find images of "double serpents." The Aztec *Quetzalcoatl* is a plumed serpent (meaning both serpent and twin). The serpent sometimes takes the form of the dragon, which, according to *The Complete Dictionary of Symbols*, represents "the union of two opposed principles." In Greek mythology, the monster–serpent *Typhon* has the ability to touch the stars. Even the presumed founder of Taoism, Chuang-Tzu, writes of a cosmic fish–bird."[xxv] In Hindu mythology, we find *Sesha*, the thousand-headed serpent who floats on the cosmic ocean while Vishnu and Lakshmi *recline* its coils.[xxvi]

THE BRIDGE: HEALING OUR DISCONNECT

According to Narby, the symbolism of the serpent corresponds to the DNA strand. DNA, the information molecule of life, is much like the mythical serpent. In *The Cosmic Serpent,* Narby explains how DNA and its duplication mechanisms are the same for all creatures; the only thing that changes is the order of the letters. You can find this going back to the origins of life as we know it. Even the biologist Robert Pollack says that "the planet's surface has changed many times over, but DNA and the cellular machinery for its replication have remained constant."[xxvii]

At the beginning of our earth's existence about 4.5 billion years ago, the planet was uninhabitable. The earth's surface gradually began to cool, and approximately 3.9 billion years ago, a thin crust formed on the molten magma. DNA appeared soon thereafter. Scientists have found minute traces of biological activity in rocks that are 3.85 billion years old. In those first 2 billion years, the earth was filled mostly with anaerobic bacteria. Slowly, the opening up of metabolic pathways filled the atmosphere with oxygen, and life then blossomed. Around 550 million years ago, life exploded with multicellular organisms of plants and animals on both land and water. The cell-based DNA is a part of our air, our lands, and the diversity of the planet. It has multiplied into a cacophony of life while remaining unchanged. Narby calls DNA the "master of transformation."[xxviii]

Narby talks about how the shamans use this portal as a "bridge," similar to what religious historian Mircea Eliade calls the *axis mundi*. This is the passage that shamans use (often guarded by a serpent) to reach the axis, acquire knowledge, and bring back information for healing.[xxix] According to Narby, DNA-based life emits ultra-weak radio waves that can be perceived in states of defocalization (like in hallucinatory states and dreams). The DNA strand, being the shape of two entwined serpents, then comes to us in our altered states of consciousness as serpents, ladders, cords, vines, spirals, and crystals. In their visions, shamans take their consciousness down to the molecular level and gain access to information related to DNA, which they refer to as "spirits."[xxx] This means that not only do they have a priceless understanding of

13

plants and remedies, but they also have access to a source of *biomolecular knowledge* that is financially invaluable to tomorrow's science.

The shamans of Amazonia are guardians of thousands of years of knowledge accumulated in the most biologically diverse region on earth. Their shamanic visions are stored in myths, and the mythology then informs shamanism. When we threaten the rainforests, we are also threatening an entire system of knowledge. Narby compares it to burning down the oldest universities in the world and sacrificing the knowledge of future generations.

This story is not so much to promote the use of hallucinogenic substances. Nor is it to recommend that everyone should begin seeking an Ayahuasca retreat. As such retreat centers continue to pop up in the frequency of Starbucks, I do believe that it is important to use these medicines in adherence to certain standards of accountability and protocol. The brew is by no means recreational. My experience with the plant medicine involved a great deal of inner personal work, mindfulness practice, and physical cleansing. The experiences would also in turn encourage me to remain in a practice of mindfulness and healthy living. My intentions are to outline how the altered states of consciousness I experienced brought profound healing by reminding me of the sanctity of life on this planet. I rediscovered a deep connection with the natural world.

On the one hand, I felt physiologically transformed, and on the other, I was emotionally changed. I believe that as we discover how to heal the disconnect from our natural environment that many of us experience (whether through medicinal plants or a practice of spending time in nature daily), this process will revolutionize the fields of psychology, addiction, and wellness. What is important to note is that while the experience itself proved to be cathartic, it also taught me how to navigate through internal challenges. Journeys with the plant medicine can be quite intense. Growth and learning are both lifelong processes. The results I experienced required equal amounts of hard work. I was inspired to make positive changes in my life. My views on money and consumption changed. I stopped watching television. I incorporated a regular meditation practice into my life. I became more mindful. I turn to nature in some way to center myself regularly, by sitting in a park or walking on grass barefoot. I have become more grounded and aware, which has had a positive effect on relieving the anxiety I previously suffered.

The greatest lesson I learned was that we are all interrelated, and our sense of separation causes us deep suffering. There is a lot of healing that can take place by walking the bridge of reconnection through a sacred practice of eco-consciousness. Knowing we are not *separate* helps us return to our essence. When we recognize the common source of our humanity, we are able to see that we are joined in a miracle of existence. When we learn to combine our inner wealth to create outer treasures (like love), we see that a universal intelligence is available to us all and that we are linked in a pattern of creation. I realized that our world is in a state of trance, and this is negatively impacting the psychological health of our humanity. I committed to delving deeper into the root cause of this trance, and so the sacred path of eco-consciousness began. A bridge to the outer world was unveiled.

CHAPTER 2

Healing our Money Pathology

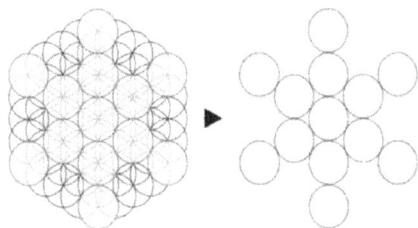

The first symbol you see is the flower of life. The pattern of thirteen circles is the fruit of life. From one to the next, a layer of wisdom is unveiled. This symbol contains a complex informational system that has been referred to as the "female gateway."[xxxi] It represents the fruits of labor and intentions. Abundance, however, comes in myriad forms (not only monetary). As you find your life's path, you find the real gift is in "as you give, so shall you receive.[xxxii]" Aligning ourselves with an examined view of prosperity is an *absolutely* crucial element of the eco-conscious path, because money is the source of suffering, stress, and dis-ease for so many in the world.

Aligning Purpose and Prosperity

I was recently reading a conversation on www.urbanbaby.com (a New York-based Internet forum devoted to anonymous discussion) in response to the question: What is your household income, and do you feel poor, middle class, upper middle class, or rich?[xxxiii] The responses were very indicative of money's inability to bring true fulfillment. They came mostly from people in New York City, with a handful of responses from other states. On average, the annual household income was in the $350k range. A large percentage of respondents with a ~$350k income stated that they either felt middle class, with some even saying they felt poor. These people commented about their struggle to keep up and get by. Even the respondents with an income of $500k stated that they felt moderately poor, mostly because of their spending habits. I was astounded that even the respondents whose annual household income was between $1M and $2M claimed that they also felt poor. For one, we see how richness and poverty are merely a matter of perspective, but if we go deeper, we see that this is a mirrored reflection of how pathological we have become in relation to it.

The concept of compensation in itself has us entangled in our pathology. "Compensated" means that you have sacrificed your time by working. That's the time you've spent doing work when you could have instead done something you wanted to do. Compensation is also the word we use in lawsuits; a person seeks compensation for an injury, pain, and suffering. Visionary Charles Eisenstein, author of *Sacred Economics*, eloquently writes, "A sacred economy recognizes that human beings desire to work: they desire to apply their life energy toward the expression of their gifts. There is no room in this conception for "compensation." Work is a joy, a cause for gratitude. At its best, it is beyond price.[xxxiv]"

In his book, Eisenstein describes the course money has taken, from the ancient gifting economies to our modern-day capitalism. He discusses how modern capitalism has contributed to alienation, competition, and scarcity. It has destroyed our sense of community and necessitated endless growth. He talks about how critical it is for us to transition to a more connected, ecological, and sustainable way of achieving economic growth. The money system *has* to change to embody this transition. He writes, "Today we are transitioning into a time that realizes the truth of the connected self, in which not only my well-being, but my very existence, my very being-ness, depends on the well-being and indeed the existence of all other beings on the planet.[xxxv]"

Our concept of money has us believing that in order to have more of it, someone else must have less of it. It brings up feelings of separation, because we think that a person can only share money if they end up having more of it in return. This is a worldview that creates competition, anxiety, and the polarization of wealth. "More for me is less for you" is the motto of the ego based on the separate self of modern economics. When our sense of self expands to include others, through love, then this shifts to "More for you is also more for me." This is the essential truth embodied in the world's authentic spiritual teachings, from Jesus' "As you do unto others, so also you do unto yourself[xxxvi]" to the Buddhist doctrine of *karma*. Understanding these teachings is not enough, as many of us exist in a divide between what we believe and what we live. A transformation in the way we experience *being* is necessary, and such a transformation usually comes about through a collapse of an old paradigm and the birth of a new one. The mature, connected self of interbeingness creates a balance between giving and receiving. In that state, you give according to your abilities and, linked with others of like spirit, you receive according to your needs. Our current monetary system was at one point perfect for humanity's growth stage of dominance and mastery. We are now, however, stepping into a new phase of cocreative partnership with our earth.

The Struggles of the Amazon

In 2009, I founded a nonprofit with a mission to merge some of the most ancient wisdom of the world's "old growth cultures" with a modern-day guide to living, in a way that recovers and recycles the sacred. During that time, I visited the region of the Amazonian rainforest between Ecuador and Peru with an organization called The Pachamama Alliance. I connected with the Achuar tribe living in the region. I came to learn a great deal of the history of the area and the struggles of the people there.

The rainforests of the Amazon basin cover an area larger than the continental United States. Nearly one-fifth of the world's fresh water is generated in the Amazon basin. The Amazon River has more than 1,100 tributaries, of which 17 are longer than 1,000 miles. Since half of every tree is made of carbon, the region serves as a sink for billions of tons of carbon within its three million square miles of thick forest and vegetation. One quarter of all modern pharmaceuticals are derived from plants in the rainforest from an area covering less than 7% of the earth's surface. However, less than 1% of rainforest plants have been studied for their medicinal properties. Indigenous cultures in the Amazon call their home the *heart of the earth*. As the heart of *our* earth, the Amazon is a massive engine that pumps hot air and vapor that feed trade winds and drive wind and rainfall around the planet. The Amazon is an *integral* part of the life-support system of our planet.

The statistics provided by the United Nations Environment Program show that the Amazon rainforest is being destroyed at a rate of approximately seven football fields per minute.[xxxvii] These forests could disappear by the end of this century with devastating consequences for our earth. Extractive industries seeking oil, minerals, and timber are fragmenting, polluting, and destroying a jewel, thereby threatening the survival of millions of people who live in the region. This is devastating for global warming. The oil, gas, or coal releases carbon stored in the earth into the atmosphere. The forests are cut down and degraded. Access roads for mines, pipelines, and oil operations are then exploited by (legal and illegal) logging interests along with settlers who use the roads to land-grab and begin the slash-and-burn process. Carbon from both above and below ground contributes to the worsening of the greenhouse effect.

Many of the region's indigenous peoples depend on the forest for their survival. They are the first to feel the full force of environmental destruction and the violations of their individual and collective rights. Prospecting for oil began in the Ecuadorian rainforest in the 1960s. Twenty-five years of oil exploration and production (where outmoded and US-outlawed drilling practices were employed) resulted in the dumping of 18 billion gallons of toxic waste directly into the rivers and onto the ground. To this day, one thousand dump sites (unfenced and untreated) still leak their toxins into the rivers and streams. The area has been described as one of the world's most contaminated industrial sites. Communities are facing extinction. The Tetete have disappeared entirely, and the Cofan, Siona, Secoya, and Huaorani peoples are all on the verge of extinction.

Having watched the history of oil companies in the northern areas, the indigenous communities in southern Ecuador have resisted oil exploitation and continue to live traditionally in some of the last pristine areas of the Ecuadorian Amazon where vast areas remain roadless and intact. Through lawsuits, nonviolent resistance, land tilting, and international alliances, these communities have been fighting to block the entry of oil companies since the mid-1990s. These indigenous groups have become leaders, winning against insurmountable odds. Their struggle is essential not only for their own survival but also for that of our entire planet.

Among these leaders in preservation are the Achuar (meaning "the people of the *aguaje palm*"). The Achuar are an indigenous culture of the Amazon rainforest of some 4,500 individuals along either side of the border between *Ecuador* and *Peru*. As of the early 1970s, the Achuar were one of the last of the *Jivaroan* groups still to be spared the effects of Western contact in southern Ecuador.[xxxviii] Visiting the Achuar territories of the southern Ecuadorian Amazon, I learned of the Achuar people's long history of opposition to petroleum exploration and extraction and of their struggle to protect their rights, their homelands, and their cultures. The southern Ecuadorian Amazon contains some of the country's largest surviving areas of primary tropical rainforest.

Home to the Shuar, Achuar, and Kichwa peoples, this region has been under threat from the oil industry for the past decade. Southern Ecuadorian indigenous communities are aware of the destruction in the northern Amazon and have continued their nonviolent resistance to oil drilling in their territories. They know that if their lands are opened up for oil exploitation, the rainforest will be destroyed by roads and pipeline infrastructure, which would then pave the way for settlers, poachers, and illegal loggers. The rainforest would be polluted, deforested, and severely degraded.

The Ecuadorian government has currently divided nearly 10 million acres of south-central Amazon rainforest for oil exploitation. Having twice extended the deadline for oil companies and investors to bid on this area of rainforest in 2013, three bids on four separate blocks were brought in on November 28, 2013. Ecuador's government was left with fewer bids than hoped for[xxxix]. The struggle continues today, as the Ecuadorean government reviews their received bids.

Connecting with the Achuar gave me the opportunity to spend time with a group of people who still live and care for two million acres of pristine rainforest where no roads have yet been built. Their lifestyle is highly influenced by a dream culture. They wake up early in the morning to tell their dreams to their family. They make important decisions in their life according to the wisdom of their dreams. After dream sharing, the elders tell myths to their children. The Achuar's oral tradition has kept all their collective wisdom alive for thousands of years.

The Achuar remind us of our interconnected world and the importance of honesty and sharing. There is enough for everyone. Women and men have different tasks for the survival of the family and community. Women's roles are usually domestic and include duties such as gathering food and preparing meals. Men work in the forest and hunt; they also make tools that they use for hunting (blowguns and traps). Gardens (*chacras*) are taken care of by women only. The chacras contain large quantities and varieties of plant species, but their value is much greater than merely a source of food. The Achuar shared with me that their chacras are also sanctuaries for women, where they express their grief and suffering (in private) since public displays of emotion are not usually encouraged. Women also give birth to their children in the chacras.

In the early 1990s, the Achuar began to have dreams of a threat that was about to destroy their home and traditional ways of life.

They knew from their contact with neighboring tribes that their home was in danger of being taken over by the oil companies in the region. At the same time, they were influenced by an ancient prophecy of the eagle and condor. This prophecy tells of a moment in history when the eagle (represented by intellect and the mind) would come together with the condor (represented by wisdom and the heart) to ensure a continued existence for humankind. The Achuar decided to reach out to the world that threatened their existence. In the mid-1990s, through a mysterious set of circumstances, a group of North Americans visited the remote and intact group of indigenous people.

This relationship, which was to become The Pachamama Alliance, was initiated by the indigenous elders and shamans themselves who, out of their deep concern for the growing threat to their ancient way of life and their recognition that the roots of this threat lay far beyond their rainforest home, actively sought the partnership of committed individuals living in the modern world. The Achuar shared their vision of the urgency for us to change the dream of the modern world and stated that the most important thing we can do is to awaken from a dream that values overconsumption to one that values and sustains life.

The indigenous people of South America have referred to our modern worldview as a "dream." One of the most powerful actions that can be taken in support of the rainforest and its inhabitants is to "change the dream of the North" since it is our dream (our desires and consumptive appetites) that is driving the destruction of the rainforests around the world. Ultimately, to assure the long-term survival of our rainforests, and indeed of the natural world (and even ourselves), we need to address the core values and ways of seeing the world that are deeply embedded in our modern worldview.

Conscious Currency Creation

To me, no one has captured the energetics of money in quite the way that Lynne Twist has. As well as being cofounder of The Pachamama

Alliance, she also founded The Soul of Money Institute. She has worked with over 100,000 people in 50 countries in the arenas of fundraising with integrity, conscious philanthropy, strategic visioning, and in examining our views about money.

Lynne Twist teaches that we must delve deeply into the core of how we view money. Too often, we compromise and dismiss our truth in our relationship with money. This occurs in the way we use it, acquire it, give it away, or avoid it. In order to heal the relationship we have with money, we must align ourselves to it in a way that frees us and enables us to live according to our integrity and the full expression of our authenticity.

Money, as a concept, was created more than 3,500 years ago to facilitate the sharing and exchange of goods and services.[xl] If at one point it was a tool, today we have assigned it the power to become one of the single most important aspects of our lives. We sacrifice our health and relationships for it. Money, for most, is not a place of freedom and clarity. The decisions we make in our lives are unfortunately ruled by it. Because of the power we give to money, it is very easy to disconnect from the essence of who we are. We often act in ways that aren't in alignment with our core values. Our paradigm of money has resulted in a separation of who we are: our inner and outer selves. It becomes difficult to integrate these two aspects. Often, to make a living, we ruin our health and kill a part of our souls in the process.

The good news is that money can be positive and transformative. It can bring in line your skills and strengths with your highest aspirations. We can begin to have a good relationship with it, and it's actually absolutely imperative that we do so. Money then becomes an arena in which we engage in meaningful practice day in and out. Unfortunately, the drive for money—because we feel we either don't have enough or need more of something—is what rules our soul.

Marketers use this exact psychology when targeting consumers. If you think about it, all goods and services can basically be divided into two groups: one that targets a need and the other that targets a desire. Marketers count on the feeling of not having enough, which is easy because it's a default setting in our brains. "Not enough" becomes a seat of fear that controls our lives. We look to everything we can to fulfill this need or desire, and we become very disconnected from the highest value of our souls. We are on the receiving end of an endless stream of seductions that hope to make us buy. Even the wealthiest people in the world are plagued by feelings of wanting more. When we live from the perspective of "not enough," everything in our lives becomes an expression of this. We can, however, make the choice to not "buy into it." More is not always better. Money is not the value our own self-worth.

I recently had an opportunity to help a friend of mine who was selling a house for a divorced woman. This divorcée had sued her husband for all his assets and then sued her own attorney. She was as litigious as they come. She was selling a house she had bought for herself post-divorce. For a woman living on her own, she lived in an almost two-million-dollar home with more space and more luxury than anyone could ever need. She was selling this house for just under $1.7M. I assisted my friend in her communications with this woman.

The divorcée was bitter, angry, terribly unhappy, and addicted to pharmaceuticals. My friend feared that, at some point, she might try to sue her too. The client was nearly impossible to reason or communicate with, and when the house was finally about to be sold, she became increasingly manic. She didn't want to spend the $480 the buyers had requested to fix a vent pre-closing. My friend ended up covering the costs of these minor repairs. This woman, who had accumulated most of her wealth through litigation and was unhappy about having to spend $480 on a repair for the sale of an almost $1.7M home, revealed a lot about the consciousness of our society. Here was a woman who was so lonely that she felt the need to fill her life with "things" to feel better. The things never really made her feel better, and she continued to feel angry and resentful. Her pathology is representative of the pathology of our world today.

Healing comes when we transform the way we view money into a way that values integrity. We use money to express value rather than undermine it. We begin to work from a place of wholeness, rather than from a place of longing. We feel a natural calling to share our resources in a way that serves our highest commitment. This is the place of truth, and when we let go of the need to make more money, we free up energy to focus on the valuable aspects of our business. We move from a fear-based paradigm and align ourselves with one that embraces all possibility in life.

In the book *Soul of Money*, Pachamama Alliance cofounder, Lynne Twist, talks about how money is like water[xli], "Money flows through all our lives, sometimes like a rushing river, and sometimes like a trickle. When it is flowing, it can purify, cleanse, create growth, and nourish. But when it is blocked or held too long, it can grow stagnant and toxic to those withholding or hoarding it. Like water, money is a carrier. It can carry blessed energy, possibility, and intention, or it can carry control, domination, and guilt. It can be a current or currency of love—a conduit for commitment—or a carrier of hurt or harm. We can be flooded with money and drown in its excess, and when we dam it up unnecessarily, we keep it out of circulation to the detriment of others.[xlii]"

Money is indeed a carrier. We can use its power to do great things. We can use it to fulfill our highest ideals and commitments. Money can be a resource for transformation and, at its best, can be life-affirming. True wealth is measured by sharing and giving, allocating and distributing. We can choose to allow our money to flow toward projects, companies, and businesses we value and respect. For the creation of a new economic model that honors the earth, it is vital that we drop the frame of reference that competition is everything. We can no longer function on the model of economics that points us in the direction of competition equating growth. Healthy competition is important, but competition to the point of destruction is not. We need to begin to think in terms of cooperation instead. We can pass around and share what's good and build our business from the viewpoint of a worldwide community.

Money is an incredible transmitter of an intention in its manifestation to a vision of fulfillment. Look at how Mother Teresa raised tens of millions of dollars to energetically direct toward the people who were moved by her to make a difference. We all have the power to make money in much the same way. We can make a lot of money in the process of serving the larger good. Imagine the shift that would be possible if millions of people committed to capturing the money that's available out there through healing our planet. Your business of creating a better world can be a profitable venture. If we can move into a paradigm that all business needs to value sustainability, fairness, and openness toward improving the state of the world, while making a profit in the process, then we are on the right path. The new frontier of business is full of innovation, radically reimagined business models, and huge vision.

Our Economic Pathology

I've known John Perkins, who is the cofounder of The Pachamama Alliance, as an author and teacher of Shamanic studies. His book, *Confessions of an Economic Hit Man*, felt relevant to my experiences in Ecuador. As I started the book and read of Perkins' description of his drive to Shell, Ecuador, it reminded me of my journey as I made my way down the very same road from Quito to Shell and passed the 156-megawatt Agoyan hydroelectric project about which he wrote. This project, like many others, fuels the industries that make a handful of Ecuadorian families wealthy. It has been the source of untold suffering for the farmers and indigenous people who live along the river, and it has put Ecuador severely in debt while inflated numbers give US companies reason to be there in the first place.

In his book, Perkins wrote very intimately about Ecuador's Amazon region, which he first visited in 1968 when Texaco had just discovered petroleum in the region. Today, a trans-Andean pipeline, which was built shortly after 1968, still leaks over half a million barrels of oil into the jungle. Vast areas of rainforest have fallen, many animals have vanished, three Ecuadorian indigenous cultures have been driven to the point of extinction, and beautiful rivers are now flaming cesspools.

Perkins was one of the world's leading economists for many years. He worked directly with the heads of the World Bank, the

International Monetary Fund (IMF), and other global financial institutions. Around twenty years ago, Perkins quit his work in this field because he realized it was morally and ethically wrong to create a world empire at the expense of the less advantaged. He explains in detail how he created economic projections for countries to accept billions of dollars in loans they couldn't afford. He calls himself the "economic hit man," which he describes as, "A highly paid professional who cheats countries around the globe out of trillions of dollars. Perkins describes how economic hit men funnel money from the World Bank, the US Agency for International Development (USAID), and other foreign aid organizations into the accounts of huge corporations, and the pockets of a few wealthy families who control the planet's natural resources. They play a game as old as empire, one that has taken on new dimensions during this time of globalization.[xliii]"

As an economist for the international consulting firm *Chas. T. Main*, Inc. (MAIN), he was told in confidential meetings that he had two primary objectives. The first was to justify huge loans for countries. These loans would be for major engineering and construction projects, which were to be carried out by MAIN and other US companies, such as Bechtel, Halliburton, Stone & Webster, and Brown & Root. The second was to help bankrupt the countries that received these loans after the US companies that were involved had been paid. This would ensure that these countries would remain in debt to their creditors and would then be easy targets when the US needed favors such as military bases, United Nations (UN) votes, and access to natural resources such as oil.[xliv]

Perkins' job was to produce economic growth projections that would make the case for a variety of major projects. If the US decided to lend a country money, Perkins would compare the economic benefits of different projects, such as power plants or telecommunications systems. He would then produce reports that showed the economic growth the country would experience as a result of these projects. These economic growth projections needed to be high enough to justify the loans; otherwise, the loans would be denied. Gross national product (GNP) was always the most important factor in these economic projections. The project expected to increase the GNP the most would be chosen.

In the cases in which there was only one project under consideration, it needed to be shown that it would greatly benefit the GNP. GNP figures can be quite deceptive. Perkins says, "The growth of GNP may result even when it profits only one person, such as an individual who owns a utility company, while the majority of the population is burdened with debt."[xlv] All these projects were meant to make huge profits for the contractors. The US engineering and construction companies involved would be assured of great wealth. At the same time, a few wealthy families and influential leaders in the receiving countries would become very happy and very rich thanks to these loans. The leaders of these countries would also have bolstered political power because they would be credited with bringing industrial parks, power plants, and airports to their people. The problem is that these countries could not handle the debt of these loans, and their poorest citizens were the people deprived of health, education, and other social services as these countries struggled economically to overcome their huge debts.

Meanwhile, the huge American media conglomerates portray these projects as favors being provided by the United States. American citizens generally have no trouble believing these messages, and they are led to perceive these actions as unselfish acts of international goodwill. Ultimately, due to the large debts, the US is able to draw on these countries for political, economic, and military favors whenever desired. Of course, the US corporations involved with the expensive projects become extremely wealthy.[xlvi]

It was during the 1960s that we saw the empowerment of international corporations and multinational organizations, such as the World Bank. This allowed for governments, corporations, and multinational organizations to form mutually beneficial relationships. United States intelligence agencies were able to use these relationships to their advantage. Government organizations, such as the National Security Agency (NSA), were now able to screen for potential economic hit men (as they did with Perkins) and then have them hired by international corporations, such as MAIN.[xlvii] Perkins writes, "These economic hitmen would never be paid by the government; instead, they would draw their salaries from the private sector. As a result, their dirty work, if exposed, would be chalked up to corporate greed rather than to government policy. In addition, the corporations that hired them, although paid by government agencies and their multinational banking counterparts (with taxpayer money), would be insulated from congressional oversight and public scrutiny, shielded by a growing body of legal initiatives, including trademark, international trade, and Freedom of Information laws.[xlviii]"

Perkins would go on to head major projects all over the world. However, he could not stop struggling with his conscience over the negative outcomes he believed he was causing as an Economic Hit Man. In 1978 and 1979, the consequences of EHM empire building became clear to Perkins when he saw what happened in Iran. While the US had supported the shah, the results had led to class wars and passionate animosity toward the "corporatocracy" being implemented in Iran.

Perkins had seen this hostility firsthand in several of the countries where he had helped to create similar situations with his EHM practices. The citizens of these countries hated US policy and blamed it for their corrupt leaders and despotic government. In Iran, the situation escalated and led to the shah fleeing the country for his own safety and Iranians storming the US Embassy and taking 52 hostages (remember the movie *Argo*?). It was then that Perkins fully realized that the United States was a nation denying the truth about its imperialist role in the world, and he became overwhelmed with guilt over his role in this global movement. Perkins sank into depression and quit his job at MAIN in 1980.

Perkins his book post-9/11 when he knew he could no longer wait and felt he had to expose these practices and the consequences they create. He has said that we have, "convinced ourselves that all economic growth benefits humankind, and that the greater the growth, the more widespread the benefits.[xlix]"

The Prophecy of the Condor and the Eagle

In his books, Perkins writes about the Prophecy of the Condor and the Eagle. Many of the world's ancient wisdom traditions talk about how we entered a period of transition in the late 1990s. Human societies took two different paths before this period. One was the path of the condor (representing the heart), and the other was the path of the eagle (representing the brain). The prophecy said that in the 1490s, the two paths would converge and the eagle would drive the condor out of extinction. Five hundred years later, a new epoch would begin in which the condor and the eagle would have the same path. If they accepted the opportunity to merge, this would create a remarkable offspring. Symbolically this speaks of the merging of the world's indigenous traditions with the technologies of science. It is the balancing of yin and yang and the bridging of the north and the south.[1]

The powerful message is that we have entered a time when we can benefit from the diverse ways of seeing ourselves and the world and can use them as a springboard to higher awareness. The condor people of the Amazon teach us that if we are to address questions about the nature of what it is to be human in the twenty-first century and face our commitment to the next decades, we must also open our eyes and examine the consequences of our actions. We live in the most powerful nation history has ever known, and we spend our time worrying about reality shows, football, balance sheets, and the stock market. Instead, we must reevaluate who we are and the type of world we want for our children.

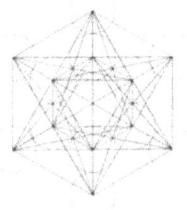

The Prophecy of the Condor and the Eagle reminds me of Metatron's Cube. The geometry of the symbol is the place where female and male energies combine to create something entirely new. By beginning with the thirteen female circles from the Fruit of Life, and connecting every center with straight male lines, a cube-like shape appears. You can see the five Platonic solids when focusing on the lines. The joining of yin and yang creates substance, form, harmony, and creativity. This merging is where creative solutions emerge to our challenges. Focusing on Metatron's Cube is a metaphor for problem solving in three-dimensional reality. Like the prophecy, it teaches us that we can merge disparate aspects of humanity and, when held in equilibrium, can create a balanced whole. Bringing this symbol into the way in which we view money can help us balance the contributions we make in giving life, substance, justice, and freedom to the community as a whole.

CHAPTER 3

Healing the Modern World Trance

The trinity teaches us that we are not only divine soul and physical body but also the consciousness that is the source of both. It is a symbolic aspect of the blueprint structuring our reality. The trinity in us can be seen as the two halves of our brain with the pineal gland, or the two halves of our psyche with the consciousness that experiences them. It is the spirit from which our mind and body have their origin, forming the mind–body–spirit trinity. It is the child within us who never separated into masculine or feminine, representing the perfect balance of the two.

Through symbols, these stories and ideas remind us that we are an infinite consciousness that is our unchanged truth. When we look out at the duality of the world (light and dark, hot and cold), it's easy to view the dualistic "two," forgetting the unified "one" from which we arose. Similarly, we view a separation of our isolated ego self from the world, which is another duality. The third represents the simultaneously existing one consciousness experiencing all the dualistic creations and the unity between them. The third is a recognition of ourselves as witnesses of the self, which is all consciousness. The state of the "one" experiencing the "two" is the *trinity of creation*. As we ascend from duality to unity, we move from separation to unification. When we move from separation to unity, we begin the process of our healing.

The Modern World Trance

> *If you are coming to help us, you are wasting your time. But if you are coming because your liberation is bound up with ours, then let us work together.*
>
> —INDIGENOUS ELDER

The Pachamama Alliance's "Awakening the Dreamer: Changing the Dream" symposium was a response to the request from the Achuar to return to our homes and help change the dream of the modern world. They wanted citizens of the modern world to help them spread their message that it is our overconsumption—our reliance on fossil fuels—that threatens to not only destroy them but us as well. The key features of the symposium are a deep contemplation of the following four questions:

- **Where Are We?** (An examination of the state of environmental, social, and personal well-being)
- **How Did We Get Here?** (Tracing the root causes of our current imbalance)
- **What's Possible for the Future?** (Discovering new ways of relating with each other, with the earth, and looking at the emerging movement for change)
- **Where Do We Go from Here?** (Considering the stand we want to take in the world and our personal and collective impact)

The symposium pushed me to reexamine the assumptions in my own life. I feel it is fundamentally important to share this part of my journey with you. It offers empowering insights into where we are now. Embracing, understanding, and acknowledging the current state of the world is essential to the sacred path of eco-consciousness. We learn that we are not separate but are connected on both the micro and macro levels.

I. WHERE ARE WE?

For thousands of years, population growth progressed at a steady rate. Then, about 200 years ago, came the dawning of the Industrial Revolution. The Industrial Revolution started in the mid-1700s in Great Britain when machinery began to replace manual labor. Fossil fuels replaced the wind, water, and wood used primarily for the manufacture of textiles and the development of iron-making processes. This trend spread throughout Europe and North America. This transformation is referred to as the *industrialization of the world*. This then led to sweeping increases in production capacity. The *Industrial Revolution* marked a major turning point in our ecology and our relationship with the environment. It changed every aspect of human life. The impact on our world, however, would not begin to register until the early 1960s (some 200 years later).

The effects on human development, health, social welfare, consumption of natural resources, energy usage, and sanitation were tremendous. Not only did society develop the ability to have more things faster, but it also developed higher-quality things. The *Industrial Revolution's* most prolific effect on the modern world was in the form of worldwide population growth.

Modern humans have been around for about 2.2 million years. By the dawn of the first millennium (AD), it is estimated that the total world human population was 150–200 million, growing to 300 million in the year 1,000. At the dawn of the Industrial Revolution in the mid-1700s, the world's human population grew by about 57% to 700 million. It would reach one billion in 1800. In the 100 years after the onset of the Industrial Revolution, the world population grew by 100% to two billion people in 1927 (about 1.6 billion by 1900). During the twentieth century, the world population grew to about six billion people. Since the 250 years from the beginning of the

Industrial Revolution to today, the world population has increased by approximately six billion people.[li]

Human population growth is indelibly tied to the increased use of natural and man-made resources, land, and an increase in waste byproducts to be disposed. *This exponential population growth* led to growing requirements for resources, energy, food, housing, and land, as well as an exponential increase in waste byproducts. Looking back at the beginning of the Industrial Revolution, one can clearly see the effects of the principle of environmental unity (change in one system causes change in others). Seeds of progress were planted during that time, and now we are facing the ramifications of those planted seeds. Progress has also brought about changes to our ecology.

Environmental Sustainability

Sustainability is about meeting or exceeding the needs of the present without compromising the ability of future generations to meet or exceed their own needs. Today, our earth is under severe stress. We are putting such a strain on the earth that the ability to sustain our future generations cannot be taken for granted. Every habitat around the world is currently being depleted. We have deforestation, soil erosion, the polluting of our rivers and oceans, overfishing, the toxic burdens on our physiologies, and rates of stress and disease skyrocketing.

In 2007, the earth's people used about 50% more natural resources than the planet could regenerate.[lii] The ecological footprint is a measure of human demand on the Earth's *ecosystems*. It is a standardized measure of demand for *natural capital* that may be contrasted with the planet's *ecological* capacity to regenerate.[liii] It represents the amount of biologically productive land and ocean area necessary to supply the resources a human *population* consumes and to assimilate associated waste.

Using this assessment, it is possible to estimate how much of the earth (or how many earths) it would take to support humanity if everyone followed a given lifestyle. The WWF's *Living Planet Report 2010* found that in 2007, the global ecological footprint was 18 billion hectares. This means that the earth's people needed 18 billion hectares of productive land to provide each person with the resources required to support his or her lifestyle and to absorb the wastes he or she produced. Unfortunately, there were only 11.9 billion global hectares available. This means that in 2007, people used about 50% more natural resources than the planet could regenerate.[liv] The message is clear: We need to consume less if we are to live within the regenerative capacity of the earth.

A report published by the Organization for Economic Cooperation and Development (OECD) projects a picture of what the world will look like in 2050, based on current global trends. In the report, it is estimated that in 2050, we will be a population of 9.2 billion people, generating a global GDP four times that of current GDP and requiring 80% more energy. We will still be mostly 85% reliant on fossil fuels by that time.[lv] The report warns that the result will be the "locking in" of global warming, with a rise of as much as 6°C (about 10.8°F) predicted by the end of the century. Combined with the effects of population growth on biodiversity, water, and health, the report asserts that the ensuing environmental degradation will result in consequences "that could endanger two centuries of rising living standards."[lvi]

According to the report, the urban centers of the world will bear the brunt of the population growth, with 70% of the world's people living in towns and cities by 2050, compared to just over 50% today. The towns and cities with fewer than half a million inhabitants today will grow most rapidly by 2050. It is thought that GDP growth rates in India and China will slow as drivers of growth, such as education, converge with those of the developed world. A quarter of the population of the OECD (consisting of 34 countries[lvii]) will be over 65 by the middle of the century, and the populations of India and China will also age significantly. It is predicted that China's workforce will actually shrink. The populations of Japan and Korea, as well as parts of Europe, will decline. This trend is not expected to be mirrored in the US and Canada, where immigration is projected to keep the populations growing. In the period between 2030 and 2050, Sub-Saharan African countries will see the highest economic growth rates in the world (at approximately 6% per year). The boom will be spurred in part by rapid growth in Africa's youthful populations, although the continent will remain the least wealthy in the world.

Population growth will exacerbate the increasing needs of energy consumption. The 80% increase predicted by 2050 translates to a total global energy consumption of 900 exajoules (EJ) per year (9 x 1020 joules), which is equivalent to 65 times the annual energy consumption of the US in 2009. The report predicts that, as a direct result of increased energy consumption, there will be a 70% increase in energy-oriented carbon dioxide emissions and an overall increase of 50% in greenhouse gas emissions. This would correlate to a rise in global average temperature between 3°C and 6°C above preindustrial levels. Air pollution will overtake contaminated water and lack of sanitation as the prime causes of premature mortality across the globe, potentially rising to 3.6 million deaths per year (mostly in China and India). Death rates caused by ground-level ozone among OECD countries are projected to be among the world's highest, in part due to the aging, urbanized populations.[lviii]

Population growth has more direct effects on the environment. The world's natural resources are set to undergo unprecedented strain. Water demand is projected to grow by 55% by 2050 (including a 400% rise in manufacturing water demand), and 40% of the global population will live in "water-stressed" areas. The report identifies groundwater depletion as the greatest threat to both agricultural and urban water supplies. Nutrient pollution of water sources is projected to further deplete aquatic biodiversity. Though the number of people with access to an "improved" water source should increase, the report projects that by 2050, 1.4 billion people will be without basic sanitation.[lix]

With a need to feed more than nine billion people, farmland coverage is set to increase worldwide, placing extra pressure on land resources. It is predicted that the earth's forests will shrink by 13% and that global biodiversity will diminish by 10%. A more silent threat to human health identified in the report is the increasing danger posed by hazardous chemicals, as chemical production increasingly relocates to developing countries where safety measures are "insuffi-

HEALING THE MODERN WORLD TRANCE

cient." The report argues that immediate action makes environmental and economic sense. The status quo is no longer acceptable.

When we live in the microcosms of our suburban jungles, it's easy to not think about the consequences that the trance of the modern world is having on our planet. Individualistically, the planet seems large enough for us to not have to think about the issues outside of our bubbles; but our future is in peril. Approximately one billion people live in abject poverty. One in seven lives in slum settlements, and by 2020, the statistic will be one in three. We are living way beyond our ecological means and using the resources that our children will need in the future.[lx]

Today, we are already using about half of the world's "net primary productivity," which means we humans are using about 50% of all life on earth. We're so busy continuously sucking up the "net primary productivity" that by 2050, half the species on earth may be gone forever. We're beginning to run out of resources, and we rely too heavily on nonrenewable resources. We may have already passed the peak of oil production, and chances are great that if you're under the age of thirty as you read this, you'll probably experience a post-oil civilization in your lifetime.

What happens if we don't start making a change today? Ecologically, the scientific community is converging on a figure of about twenty-five years from now before we spiral out of control. If we don't commit to deep and lasting change by 2050, we're setting ourselves up for planetary catastrophe. We need to create a new model of environmental sustainability and sustainable prosperity.

To make matters worse, we here in the United States continue to swim in our consumer excesses. We set the prime example for the rest of the world, who see how we live on their TVs, and all of a sudden they're aspiring to the same excesses. Very few people in this world are happy with what they have. Most of us want more. Then again, it's hypocritical for us to turn around to the remaining two-thirds of the world living below poverty and tell them that they can't aspire to the luxuries we come to expect as normal.

We need to create a system in which prosperity can be delivered to everyone without destroying the earth. If we follow the logic of the

39

environmental Kuznets curve, we can say that we need to grow rich first because, with money, we will be able to invest in more efficient and less environmentally damaging technologies. Unfortunately, this isn't a replicable model. The world's growing population just can't attain our Western level of living by following conventional paths to development. The resources that would be required are too vast and too damaging to the global ecosystem. We need a new model.

We are also in the midst of a worldwide mass extinction. According to scientific analysis compiled by the World Wildlife Fund, the rapid loss of species we are seeing today is estimated by experts to be between 1,000 and 10,000 times higher than the natural extinction rate.[lxi] These experts calculate that between 0.01% and 0.1% of all species will become *extinct* each year. If the low estimate of the number of species out there is true (that there are around 2 million different species on our planet[lxii]) then between 200 and 2,000 extinctions occur every year.[lxiii] If the upper estimate of species numbers is true (that there are 100 million different species coexisting with us on our planet), then between 10,000 and 100,000 species are becoming extinct each year. Referred to as the sixth extinction crisis, unlike the mass extinction events of geological history, the current extinction challenge is one for which we, as a human species, are wholly responsible. Life itself hangs in the balance at this very moment. We lament the loss of people we love in our lives and the animals we are close to; how can we live and not lament the permanent loss of life itself?

Social Justice

A socially just world is a world in which we would be perfectly confident no matter what lot we drew in life, and every person would have a decent shot at living the best life possible. Social justice gives people the opportunity to fulfill their potential and to be treated with equal dignity. Our social contract is that we are part of a worldwide, mutually interdependent society.

How does our current global situation measure up in terms of global justice? Currently, the income gap between the rich and the poor is widening, especially in the United States. A new study shows that income inequality in America is at a record high. According to an analysis of tax filings, the income gap between the richest 1% of Americans and the other 99% widened to unprecedented levels in 2012. The top 1% of US earners collected more than 19% of household income, breaking a record previously set in 1927. Income inequality in the United States has been growing for almost three decades.[lxiv] In the documentary *Inequality for All*, Clinton Labor Secretary, Robert Reich, says, "Of all developed nations, the United States has the most unequal distribution of income, and we're surging towards even greater inequality." In 1978, according to Reich, a "typical male worker" made $48,302, while the typical top 1% earned $393,682 (more than eight times as much). In 2010, even as overall GDP and productivity increased, the average male worker's wage fell to $33,751. Meanwhile, the average top 1% earner was making more than $1.1 million (32 times that of the average earner).[lxv]

A recent *New York Times* article states that *income inequality* has soared to the highest levels since *the Great Depression* , and that the recession has done little to reverse this trend, with the top 1% of earners taking 93% of the income gains in the first full year of the recovery.[lxvi] "Growth becomes more fragile in countries with high levels of inequality like the United States," said Jonathan D. Ostry of the IMF, whose research suggests that the widening disparity since the 1980s might reduce the nation's economic expansion by as much as a third. The IMF conclusion was that, in the long run, reducing inequality and bolstering growth might be "two sides of the same coin."[lxvii]

Although the United States is among the richest countries in the world, many areas the United States are backward for advanced nation standards. Infant and maternal mortality are the highest among advanced nations, as is the *mortality rate of children under the age of 20*[lxviii] Life expectancy (at birth and at age 60) is among the lowest. Teenage pregnancy rates are not only higher than in other rich nations but are also higher than in Kazakhstan and Burundi. The United States has the highest rate of children living with a single parent among the industrialized nations in the OECD.[lxix] Within the organization, only in Turkey, Mexico, and Poland do more *children live in poor homes.*[lxx]

Beyond income statistics, inequality in this country is everywhere. For example, wealthy families invest more in their children's education, while opportunities are stacked against the poor and middle class. Sixty percent of disadvantaged children go to disadvantaged schools with fewer and lower-quality resources, according to *a report on educational disparities.*[lxxi] Literacy is more lopsided than in most other industrial nations, according to international tests of 15 year olds carried out by the OECD. The gap between the top American scorers (in the ninetieth percentile of the distribution) and those in the middle is the size of the gap between the average score in the United States and Azerbaijan.

In a society in which education has become a central determinant of economic success, the prosperity of American children is more dependent on the prosperity of their parents *than that of children in most other advanced countries.*[lxxii] The United States has the 17th-highest *poverty rate in the OECD,*[lxxiii] measured as the share of people who make do with less than half the median income. If the same variable is measured after taking into account the effect of taxes and government spending programs, the American poverty rate jumps to the fifth worst. The United States ranks among the bottom third of nations in the OECD in terms of *outlays on social programs*, such as unemployment insurance and day care, to help families deal with economic stress.[lxxiv] For many people born into privilege, we live by a premise called "the right not to know." If we have everything we want, why do we have to know beyond that? We need to know because inequality makes an economy inefficient and unstable, limits the opportunities and mobility of its citizens, and affects us all.

The Psychological Health of Humanity

There is a great loneliness of spirit in the world that is driving us to consumption, addiction, stress, and disease. The truth is that most of us are trying to live and cope in a world in which we do see the overwhelming evidence of what's happening. We have become paralyzed, believing that who we are does not matter and that there is no hope for change. We live our lives in this context of paralysis. Every one of us yearns for a connection. We want that feeling of being fully in tune with our purpose, and when we feel tension because we aren't living in a way that aligns with our highest purpose, we feel loneliness and numb it with anything we can use to force it to go away. Our loneliness has led us to a consumer-excess nightmare. Filling our lives with more things doesn't feed the hunger within the human heart. Material fulfillment doesn't necessarily equate to happiness.

Studies show that, as a society, we are becoming progressively sicker. More of us are mentally ill than in previous generations, and our mental illness is manifesting at earlier points in our lives. One study supporting this explanation took the scores of a measure of anxiety of children with psychological problems in 1957 and compared these with the scores of today's average child. Today's children (not specifically those identified as having psychological problems as did the children in 1957) are more anxious than those in previous generations.[lxxv]

Another study compared cohorts of American adults with regard to the personality trait of neuroticism, which indicates emotional reactivity and is associated with anxiety. Americans scored higher on neuroticism in 1993 than they did in 1963, suggesting that, as a population, we are becoming more anxious. When comparing the level of narcissism among cohorts of American college students between 1982 and 2006, studies indicated that more recent cohorts are more narcissistic.[lxxvi] An additional study supported the explanation that more people are diagnosed with mental illness because more of us have mental illness: The more recently an American is born, the more likely he or she is to develop a psychological disorder.[lxxvii]

According to new data from the US Substance Abuse and Mental Health Services Administration, 20% of American adults (more than 45 million people) experienced a mental illness in 2011.[lxxviii] A study by the World Health Organization shows that rates of most *mental illness* are higher in the US than in any other country in the world and that 25% of Americans have a mental disorder at some point (many of which are untreated).[lxxix]

This culture affects our children and can be seen in addiction, violence, and suicide. Violence, sexuality, race and gender stereotypes, and drug and alcohol abuse are common themes of television programs, and children in the United States watch an average of three to four hours of television a day. By the time they graduate from high school, they will have spent more time watching television than they would have spent in the classroom.[lxxx] Children spend more time watching television than they do engaging in any other activity with the exception of sleep.[lxxxi]

By age 18, a US youth will have seen 16,000 simulated murders and 200,000 acts of violence.[lxxxii] Television alone is responsible for 10% of youth violence.[lxxxiii] Research has shown that mindless television or video games may idle and impoverish the development of the prefrontal cortex, which is the portion of the brain that is responsible for planning, organizing and sequencing behavior for self-control, moral judgment, and attention.[lxxxiv]

Children and youth in North America use *4-5 times* the recommended amount of technology, often with serious consequences, according to the Kaiser Foundation 2010, Active Healthy Kids Canada 2012[lxxxv]. The study showed that technology overuse has been implicated as a causal factor in rising rates of child depression, anxiety, attachment disorder, attention deficit, autism, bipolar disorder, psychosis and problematic child behavior[lxxxvi]. Today, one in six Canadian children have a diagnosed mental illness, many of whom are on psychotropic medications[lxxxvii]. From the other side of the spectrum, as parents attach more and more to technology, they are detaching from their children. In the absence of parental attachment, detached children can attach to devices, resulting in addiction. Studies have shown that one in 11 children aged 8-18 years in North America are addicted to technology[lxxxviii].

A study conducted in the Netherlands suggests that unhappy kids are more likely to become materialistic than children who are happy with their lives. "Children who were less satisfied with their lives become more materialistic over time, but only when they are frequently exposed to advertising," said the study's lead author, Suzanna Opree. "Advertising seems to teach children that possessions are a way to increase happiness."[lxxxix] According to a United Nations Children's Fund (UNICEF) study of *child well-being, the United States ranks at the bottom* (number 20) of 21 industrial countries, beating out only Britain. With all our luxuries and wealth, American children are among the unhappiest in the world.[xc]

According to The National Eating Disorders Association and Screening for Mental Health, approximately seven million girls and women and one million boys and men struggle with eating disorders.[xci] Naomi Wolf, author of *The Beauty Myth: How Images of Beauty Are Used Against Women*, states that in the past two decades, eating disorders rose exponentially and cosmetic surgery became the fastest-growing field in the medical industry.[xcii] Our consumer spending habits doubled, pornography became the largest media category (more than other film and record categories combined), and when asked, a large number of American women told researchers that they would rather lose ten to fifteen pounds than accomplish any other goal.[xciii]

Research shows that while women have become more powerful, successful, and educated, they have become more afraid of the aging process and are quietly feeling a never-ending sense of self-dissatisfaction below the surface. Wolf says, "There is a secret 'underlife' poisoning our freedom; infused with the notion of beauty is a dark vein of self-hatred, physical obsession, terror of aging and dreaded lost control. Today, society controls us via a mass neurosis that uses food to control how we gain weight, and then feel the pressure to take it off. We are sandwiched between underweight models on our television and fast food chains down the street. Consumerism has rendered us as citizens, despite our individuality, into one massive homogenous object. We in the 21st century relate consumerism to pleasure, much to the dismay of our leaders, teachers and philosophers of yore. We have become alienated from each other, and apathetic. We are never satisfied and always lacking. We become more anxious and depressed.[xciv"]

A recent study based on Gallup's findings showed that Singapore, a country that ranks third highest according to worldwide economic measures, is the unhappiest country in the world.[xcv] Take another industrialized country like Japan, where a phenomenon known as *karōshi* (translated as death from overwork) has enough of a significant count to receive its own category among causes of death. The first case of karōshi was reported in 1969 with the death from a stroke of a 29-year-old male worker in the shipping department of *Japan*'s largest newspaper company.[xcvi] It was not until the later part of the 1980s, when several high-ranking business *executives* who were still in their prime years suddenly *died* without any previous sign of *illness*, that the *media* began picking up on what appeared to be a new phenomenon.

This new phenomenon was quickly labeled karōshi and was immediately seen as a new and serious menace for people in the *workforce*. In 1987, as *public* concern increased, the *Japanese Ministry of* Labor began to publish *statistics* on karōshi. Japan's rise from the devastation of *World War II* to *economic* prominence in the postwar decades has been regarded as the trigger for what has been called a new *epidemic*.[xcvii] Japan also happens to be the country where more benzodiazepines (for *anxiety*) are prescribed than in any other country in the world.[xcviii]

At the other end of the spectrum, the happiest people in the world are the Danes, according to the *2013 World Happiness Report* published by Columbia University's Earth Institute for the United Nations Sustainable Development Solutions Network.[xcix] The 158-page report ranks over 150 countries according to a life evaluation score that takes into account a variety of factors, such as wealth, government corruption, political freedom, and job security. Its sources include the Gallup World Poll (GWP), the World Values Survey (WVS), the European Values Survey (EVS), and the European Social Survey (ESS).

The Danes have been ranked consistently as the world's happiest people since as long ago as the early 1970s. In November 2011, they topped the happiness rankings published by the OECD. The ranking went hand in hand with a study by Green Growth Leaders, which showed that Copenhagen's green ambitions have led to a significant improvement in the quality of life of the residents of the Danish capital. The rating illustrates an ongoing trend that the superior livability offered by Denmark and Copenhagen has a significant effect on its citizens and that sustainability does perhaps go hand in hand with happiness.[c]

What strikes me as most interesting is that while both the World Happiness Report and Better Life Index almost exclusively contain wealthy nations in the top slots, a Gallup poll taken in 2012, measuring positive emotions across 148 countries claimed that Latin Americans were the happiest in the world, with eight of the top 10 countries being located in Central or South America. Like the UN report, Gallup went straight to the source, asking 1,000 people in each of the nations surveyed five questions about whether they experienced much enjoyment the day before, and if they felt respected, felt well-rested, laughed and smiled a lot, and did or learned something interesting. "These data may surprise analysts and leaders who solely focus on traditional economic indicators," Gallup researcher Jon Clifton noted. "Residents of Panama, which ranks ninetieth in the world with respect to GDP per capita, are among the most likely to report positive emotions."[ci] Although some of these countries are well-known for civil war strife, high crime, their reputation for gang violence, and lower economic indicators, their citizens are, nonetheless, known for living life in the moment, having a connection to the natural beauty of the countries, and, like Costa Rica, having a *"pura vida"* (roughly translated as "life is good") mentality.

This leads me to wonder how the mindless frenzy of waking life, which so many of us experience here in the United States, is also leading to a deep-seated disconnect from the natural world. This is the trance of the modern world about which the Achuar spoke. Many of us believe that we aren't pedaling quickly enough toward some external goal we have projected in the future. This disconnect leads us to respond to our lives with a busy-ness, overtime, extra projects, seminars, or even time at the gym. Our dissatisfaction with who we are makes us believe that we'll be happier or feel more successful if we change our appearance with weight loss, a new wardrobe, or Botox, and so we continue to focus on the ego-driven external factors that we are convinced determine our happiness.

Symbolically, Dr. Larry Dossey writes about a boat we see coming upstream toward us, veering toward the shore to rescue us. That is when we realize that we have been outrunning the very thing that could save us. That frenzied activity is, in fact, our enemy and our success and survival are often "better measured not in *busyness* and doing, but in not-doing, reflection, silence, stillness, listening, and noticing.[cii]" He talks about how often he has had patients say to him, "Cancer is the best thing that ever happened to me."[ciii]

Zen master Shunryu Suzuki writes, "Although we have no actual written communications from the world of emptiness, we have some hints or suggestions about what is going on in that world, and that is, you might say, enlightenment. When you see plum blossoms or hear the sound of a small stone hitting bamboo, that is a letter from the world of emptiness.[civ]" Yet, such presence of being is so difficult when we are always so busy doing. How often do you ask a friend how he or she has been, and he or she responds with, "So busy. Crazy busy. Busier than ever."

Americans reported in 2008 that for each consecutive year since 1987, they have been busier than the year before, with 69% reporting that they are "busy" or "very busy." When asked what they have had to give up to accommodate being busier, 56% cited sleep, 52% recreation, 51% hobbies, 44% friends, and 30% family. In 1987, 50% reported having at least one meal a day with family; by 2008, only 20% reported that this was the case.[cv] To awaken or not to awaken is no longer an option. Humanity needs more than anything right now to open ourselves to the grief and loss that has been taking place in our society. We embrace this grief through strength, with the energy to respond and become more committed and determined.

II. HOW DID WE GET HERE?

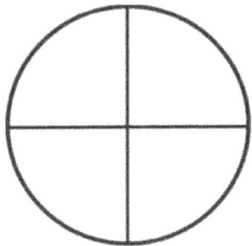

The symbol you see represents the medicine wheel. Medicine wheels act as containers of sacred space, and they are a means of connecting with the *spirit*. This embodies the symbolism of the circle with the equilateral cross. This is a reminder of our connection with nature and the movement and flow of the seasons and the heavens. Viewing ourselves as separate from nature leads to our loneliness and alienation. We are all a part of all that is. Each molecule of our being is connected to every other energetic particle in unity and oneness with everything else in the universe.

Human choices and behaviors brought us to where we are. Cosmologist and geologian Thomas Berry looked deeply at this very question. He believed that humanity was poised to embrace its role as a vital part of the larger, interdependent "communion of subjects" in the cosmos. He wrote, "First, the primary status of the universe. The universe is, 'the only self-referential reality in the phenomenal world. It is the only text without context. Everything else has to be seen in the context of the universe.' The second element is the significance of story, and in particular the universe as story. 'The universe story is the quintessence of reality. We perceive the story. We put it in our language, the birds put it in theirs, and the trees put it in theirs. We can read the story of the universe in the trees. Everything tells the story of the universe. The winds tell the story, literally, not just imaginatively. The story has its imprint everywhere, and that is why it is so important to know the story. If you do not know the story, in a sense you do not know yourself; you do not know anything.[cvi]"

We create a radical separation between humans and the natural world. Our obsession with progress makes us think that we are headed toward a future where we will master everything on earth. Our dependence on technology makes us believe that we can buy our way out of this crisis without the fundamental understanding that we are an integral part of the natural world. Our assumptions are based upon worldviews of which we are not even aware. Our actions correlate with worldviews we haven't examined. If our actions produce that which we haven't even intended, we need to know that our unexamined assumptions are producing unaware consequences. We believe our earth is there for us to satisfy our needs and desires, so we want to use the earth to make "things." This belief system has become pathological.

Each species on this planet is the result of ~13.7 billion years' worth of evolution. We all have a right to be here. We live as if we have a throwaway species, and we are swimming in unexamined assumptions. When we look and examine, we can separate ourselves from them and consciously make separate choices. Our modern worldview is not the only worldview.

There are people who are not wrapped up in progress—the intact indigenous cultures that have lived in a sustainable manner for thousands for years. They use a terminology that means "all my relations," meaning that we are related to everyone. They embody some of the most ancient wisdom on earth, which is precisely what humanity needs most right now.

As we walk through this global onset of environmental collapse, indigenous teachings remind us that what we do to the earth, we also do to ourselves. What we do to teach other, we do to the earth. Part of their wisdom comes from a traditional ecological knowledge (TEK) in which, for millennia, the indigenous people have acted as guardians of the biodiversity of our planet. They've managed relations between humans and biological cultures, with their eyes constantly on the next seven generations to come. Seven generation sustainability is an ecological concept that encourages our current generation on the planet to live sustainably and for the benefit of seven generations into the future.

This TEK has already solved many of the environmental challenges threatening us today. It's known as a sort of sacred geography of the world, where all life is animated by spirit. There is no separation between spirit and technology. We live in a world of kinship where we are all related. We learn from these cultures that true intelligence lies throughout the natural world and in the vast expanse of our universe. Because it is so vast and incomprehensible to us as humans, these cultures live humbled by the earth. The original instructions (ancient ways of living within nature) of the TEK celebrate our interconnection with one another. We remember who we are, and this encourages us to re-indigenize into our contemporary lifestyles.[cvii]

The dream of our modern world has caused us to become hypnotized by a fragmented view of the world, and we have lost our connection to the universe. We have been using the wrong operating mechanism for humanity. This, however, opens up new possibilities for the future. One way to describe our worldview is to talk about our story. This is about how our human story came to be: our values, ethics and laws. A new cultural story is emerging, and it states that we are profoundly connected on both the macro and micro levels. This is beginning to shape the consciousness of our planet and is the idea of an emergent universe.

When we begin to realize this tremendous extent of time and space, we realize that we have the capability to respond and a responsibility for the cosmology of where we live. We weren't added to the planet after the earth was assembled; rather, we came out of the earth. Nothing would exist if it were not for an incredible set of coincidences. Physicists describe the Big Bang as the birth of our universe. In that moment, the number of particles created was slightly more than the number of antiparticles. The particles and antiparticles collided and annihilated each other, filling the universe with photons. Because there was an initial imbalance, there were a few particles left after the annihilation, and this was the beginning of the material world. We, along with the stars and the rest of the universe, are leftovers from the moment of creation. The total number of particles left over was 10 to the power of 80. If the number of particles was slightly greater, gravitational forces would have forced the universe to collapse into itself. This would have formed one huge black hole, and none of us would exist. If the number of particles was slightly smaller, the universe would have expanded so quickly that there would have been no time for the galaxies to form as they did.

We are, in essence, star dust. Astronaut Rusty Schweickart once said, "From the moon, the Earth is so small and so fragile, and such a precious little spot in that Universe, that you can block it out with your thumb. Then you realize that on that spot, that little blue and white thing, is everything that means anything to you—all of history and music and poetry and art and death and birth and love, tears, joy, games, all of it right there on that little spot that you can cover with your thumb. And you realize from that perspective that you've changed forever, that there is something new there, that the relationship is no longer what it was.[cviii]" Physicists don't say that there was nothing before the Big Bang, but rather that everything came from that. In the Vedic teachings of the Upanishads, what is referred to as *samadhi* is similarly reality condensed into pure potential without dimensions, without time, and without differentiation. Samadhi isn't emptiness, though; it is *purnata*—a completeness and fullness. It consists of all time, space, causality, and states of consciousness.

Not unlike Jeremy Narby's theory of the DNA molecule holding the intelligence of creation, the Upanishads call it *sat*, where all creation is implicit as an organism is implicit in DNA or a tree in a seed. The joy of this state is pure and limitless; this is referred to as *ananda*. The message of the Upanishads is that no joy less than that of ananda can satisfy the human heart. The free, infinite, and unbounded are our natural states. We have fallen from that state and attempt to fill the void with activity. By filling the void from outside ourselves, we are making demands on life that it cannot fulfill. Finite things never satisfy infinite hunger. Only through the reunion with our Self, known as *sat-chit-ananda*, can we experience unconditional joy.

Dennis Martinez, a Native American restoration ecologist, says that humanity has never faced a global ecological collapse before, and to get through this, we are going to need the enduring knowledge of the indigenous sciences along with the best of leading-edge Western science. It is the middle way in which there is no separation between the technical and spiritual. Real intelligence dwells in the natural world and in the vast mystery of the universe, which is beyond human comprehension. In his book, *Intelligence in Nature*, Narby discovers in Japan the word for intelligence that most closely relates to the intelligence we speak of when we say it is alive and thriving in nature. This word is *chi-sei*, and Narby writes about the existence of chi-sei in all of nature. In the same way that bees can abstract rules or plants can remember and decide things, even our gut contains hundreds of millions of neurons that are capable of learning and responding to emotions. This is how, as Narby states, shamans communicate with the natural world.[cix]

Scientists who study bacteria have discovered that they are social creatures that possess unique forms of language, using chemicals to communicate with each other. Chemical communication differs, depending on the circumstance. Plants have been known to communicate with each other using odor molecules.[cx] They use chemicals to repel insects and to warn other plants of danger, enabling them to kick in their defenses. Apes, elephants, dolphins, magpies, and pigeons are able to recognize themselves in the mirror.[cxi] Elephants display compassion when they remain by the body of a deceased member of their "tribe" in a display of respect. When we move into the human realm, we see that consciousness is not confined to the brain but is a part of the universe itself.[cxii]

This ancient cosmology helps us remember who we are. Indigenous peoples have millennia-old indigenous knowledge systems (IKS) that are tribally and geographically specific. Within these teachings is TEK, which holds the memories, observations, stories, understandings, insights, and practices regarding how to follow the natural laws of a particular place. This knowledge is often encoded in the stories, songs, rituals, and daily practices of their oral traditions.[cxiii] As many of these traditions didn't have written language systems, they relied on the transmission of their knowledge through these stories, rituals, and songs. Historically, these societies have relied on subsistence farming, hunting, and gathering.

For many, TEK is foreign to the modern mindset. When we don't understand something, it is very easy for us to exoticize the "other." The indigenous traditions recognize an invisible presence throughout the world. This is a force that permeates the universe and connects everything as a living whole. The Navajo describe this as a "wind" that blows through the universe and brings the capacity for consciousness and communication with others. Our individual consciousness is part of a greater whole. Everything is connected to a *Great Spirit*, and everything should be treated with respect.

Based on their teachings, the indigenous people recognize that we are not disconnected from the larger universe. Common themes of interrelatedness emerge in all the world's sacred teachings. In the Judeo–Christian view, God reveals his name in Exodus (3:14) as "I am that I am." In the 1300s, Christian mystic Meister Eckhart wrote, "God is creating the entire universe, fully and totally, in this present now."[cxiv] In the esoteric tradition within Islam, the central doctrine of Sufism is that all phenomena are a manifestation of a single reality that arises out of unity. The thirteenth-century Sufi poet Rumi wrote in depth about the continuing arising of existence. He viewed life like a stream, writing, "It arrives new and fresh at every moment while it appears constant in its material form."[cxv]

Hinduism, which dates back 3,500 years, is the oldest of the world's living religions. It is known for its scriptures, the *Vedas*, and all Hindus believe in a supreme cosmic spirit called *Brahman*. This is the source of all things, the foundation of all existence. At the foundation of Buddha's teachings was a recognition of a moment-to-moment interdependent co-arising of all things in the universe to awaken to a reality that cannot be accessible through logic alone. The universe arises as a unified whole at each moment, and because everything arises out of everything else, everything is connected. Based on the teachings of the *Tao Te Ching*, at the heart of Taoism is the belief that Tao is the sustaining life force and mother of all things. The goal of Tao is to live in harmony with the flow of life. Even in the Western world, the philosopher Plotinus wrote (more than two thousand years ago) that, "This universe is a single living being embracing all living beings within it."[cxvi]

Within the world wisdom traditions, we see similar descriptions of the universe and a connecting life force. Merging this wisdom with the modern world means that we need to create new traditions and new ways to thrive in a complex world during intense times. Ancient wisdom has known of our interconnectedness all along—this wondrous story of "emergence." The universe evolved over the course of 14 billion years through stages of increasing complexity: preatomic, atomic, molecular, unicellular, multicellular, vertebrate, primate, and human. As cosmologist Brian Swimme once said, "Four and a half billion years ago, the Earth was a flaming molten ball of rock and now, it can sing opera."

The symbol above, called the flower of life, is one of the most universal pieces of sacred geometry that is available to us today. This figure is found "flash burned" into the walls of the Osiron (Temple of Resurrection) in Abydos, Egypt.[cxvii] The symbol is found in more than eighteen countries, from Turkey to Tibet to the Yucatán. The flower of life represents a pure life force that contains all cellular memory of humankind, the matrix of all matter. This symbol is an akashic information system containing records of all that was, all that is, and all that will be. Its message for us is to open up to the knowledge within and listen to the responses received. What comes through is the intention that wishes to see us achieve our highest good.

III. WHAT IS THE POSSIBILITY FOR OUR FUTURE?

Our current path is unsustainable and cannot last. At the same time, the way of seeing the world is changing. Can humanity really transform? Throughout time, through Darwin's theory of evolution, we have seen that, when it is required, our species transforms to enable its survival.

THE SACRED PATH OF ECO-CONSCIOUSNESS

There is a creative capacity within, that allows us to let go and forgive. If we look back at the extraordinary transformations that have occurred in human history, whether from taking a populace from rebellion against tyranny to total institutional change, we see that we are an unpredictable species. Indeed, there is a creative force in this universe to transform. There is no more exciting a time to be alive than when people are awakening to the possibilities.

When environmental activist Paul Hawken talks of the new superpower emerging on earth, he describes this as the most diverse unnamed movement the world has ever seen. It's the largest social movement humanity has seen. This movement is encouraging a generation of people, who are creating new out-of-the-box ways of doing things. It recognizes that the youth are not our future; they are our collaborators in the now.[cxviii]

To rediscover the possibilities for our future, it's important that we first understand that the most primary experience of our world is through the physical domain. This is what we consider to be the "real world." This world contains matter and objects that have firm boundaries, and things appear to be three-dimensional from this perspective. We use our senses. We see, hear, feel, taste, and smell. This real world is where time seems to flow in a straight line from past and present to future. The stories in our physical domain have a beginning, middle, and end. All that is born must die. The physical world is governed by immutable laws of cause and effect.

We perceive our world to be explainable and predictable, yet modern science is just beginning to catch up with the ancient wisdom of interconnectedness. Take, for instance, Bell's theorem of quantum physics (where no physical theory of local hidden variables can ever reproduce all the predictions of quantum mechanics), Einstein's theory of relativity, or Heisenberg's uncertainty principle. All these theories indicate that how (and even when) we look at subatomic particles affects what we see. All particles of matter, property, position, and velocity are influenced by the intention of presence of all other particles. Atoms are aware of other atoms.

Now, I'm no physicist, but I do know that at the quantum level of existence, everything consists of information and energy. At this level, we cannot perceive from the arena of our senses. Our thought, mind, and ego are levels of the quantum domain. We feel our thoughts to be real, yet they don't have a solid shape or form. Everything in the physical domain is a manifestation of the energy and information in the quantum domain. In Einstein's famous equation, $E=mc^2$, we see that E is energy and equals Mass (m) times the speed of light squared (c^2). Invisible waves of energy and information are also manifested as solid matter. Because events in the quantum domain occur at the speed of light, our senses cannot process at this speed and can only experience what we *perceive* to be reality.

Objects are perceived differently because energy waves contain different amounts of information, and this is determined by the frequency or vibration of the energy waves. Energy is coded for different information, depending on its vibration. Our physical world is nothing but information contained within energy, vibrating at different frequencies. Our senses process things more slowly. If, however, we were able to perceive everything at the quantum level, we would quickly become aware that we live in one big "energy soup."[cxix]

Each of us is a ball of energy floating in this great big soup. From one moment to the next, we come in contact with another person's energy field, and each of us will respond differently to that energy. We are expressions of energy and information. Sometimes, we may feel this as a "connection" we have to another person. We are constantly exchanging energy and information in the physical domain. At the deepest level, there is no boundary between ourselves and everything else in the world.

Physics teaches us that everything solid is made up of atoms and that the solidity we feel is from these atoms bumping against each other. An atom is a nucleus surrounded by electrons. The outer shell is not a solid, but a ring of electrons. When we touch something, we perceive it as solid because of the rings of electrons bumping against each other. Our eyes are programmed to see things in the three-dimensional domain. Whenever we touch something, our rings of electrons meet, meld, and then separate. With every encounter we have, we are exchanging bits of information and energy and walking away slightly transformed. This is interconnectedness. The solidity of our physical world exists in the field in which our senses can perceive, but because we cannot discern the waves of energy and information that make up the quantum level, it is difficult for us to perceive things from that level. When we practice fine-tuning these senses, we become aware that there are gaps in our existence and that we are holding together a sense of continuity through our memories.

There is a Zen story about two monks looking at a flag blowing in the wind. One believes that the flag is moving, yet the other thinks that the wind is moving. They ask their teacher, who tells them that they are both wrong. The teacher explains that it is consciousness that is moving, and as consciousness moves, the world is created. In much the same way, sacred ancient texts can be interpreted and translated in different ways, depending on the consciousness of the person who is interpreting them. The level of existence that consists of a consciousness and an intelligence is where energy is constantly emerging from a network of possibility. In the tradition of Vedanta, the most fundamental level of nature is neither the material domain nor energy; it is consciousness itself in the form of pure potential. It is nonlocal because it cannot be quantified by a location. The intelligence of pure potential is what translates the energetic soup into material form. It is the organizing nature behind everything.

According to metaphysicist Larry Dossey, MD, nonlocal events have three qualities that distinguish them from the physical world. They are all correlated and are either unmediated, unmitigated, or immediate.

> **Unmediated:** This is when the behavior of subatomic events is acausally interrelated. This means that one event does *not* cause another event, yet the behavior of one is correlated and connected to the other.
>
> **Unmitigated:** This is when the correlation between nonlocal events is unchanged despite distance in space and time. In the nonlocal domain, you would be able to hear someone speak, (whether you were a thousand miles away or in the same room) in a completely unchanged way.

> **Immediate:** This occurs when there is no travel time needed for a nonlocal event. There is no lag time between sound and light. Nonlocal correlations don't necessarily follow the rules of physics. Correlations that occur at this level occur immediately and instantly. There is no cause and no weakening regardless of distance.

Take this further and Minkowski's eight-dimensional hyperspace describes a level of existence where scientists conceive that the distance between two separate events (no matter how distant they are in space) is always zero. This is the dimension of existence where we are all inseparable. This place of unity is where separation is but an illusion. Observation is the key to defining the wave particle as a single entity, and physicists such as Niels Bohr believe that consciousness is responsible for the collapse of a wave particle. Without consciousness, everything would exist as undefined packets of energy, and without consciousness acting as the observer and interpreter, everything would exist in a state of pure potential. Tapping into this domain is where manifestation occurs.

Biologist Rupert Sheldrake has a theory that he calls "morphic resonance." This theory hypothesizes that an individual or group's actions, beliefs, and insights create resonances that make it more likely that other people (otherwise unconnected) will experience the same insights or experiences on their own. In the modern world, it is similar to the phenomena of radio, television, and microwave transmissions. Their signals are generated as patterns in subtle energy fields that move out in broadcast patterns. We cannot hear or see them, but with the right receiver, this pattern can be translated back into sounds and images.

Interesting experiments have been conducted to measure the electromagnetic activity of cells using an Electroencephalography (EEG) type instrumentation. Sperm and cells reacted to things that occurred in the people connected to them, even when they were miles away (known as biocommunication). The cells of biological organisms, such as plants and bacteria, have the ability to biocommunicate. Living cells have a consciousness and can communicate with other cells of the same (or different) species, even at a distance. This communication has been shown to be instantaneous regardless of distance in space. These results can only be explained from the domain of nonlocal correlation, which is what connects and orchestrates everything. This is a boundless field of energy and consciousness that is everywhere and nowhere, manifesting everything. This is where synchronicity occurs.[cxx]

Psychiatrist Carl Jung originated the notion of synchronicity. This is when seemingly unrelated events share a common meaning in the form of a "coincidence." When one of Jung's patients was recounting a dream about a golden scarab beetle, at that exact moment he heard a tapping on the window. When he opened the window, a rose chafer beetle (an insect most similar to the scarab in Jung's region) flew in. At this moment, he realized that the mythological meaning of the scarab was an Egyptian symbol of rebirth. He saw this as absolutely integral to his patient's problems. This is also why the beetle appeared in waking life.

This phenomenon indicates that we are experiencing each day flooded with fields of meaning. Each field of meaning has a vibration to it, and individuals, events, dreams, and emotions with similar vibrations will resonate with each other and recur. Deepak Chopra calls this the practice of *achieving spontaneous fulfillment of a desire*, through the harnessing of the infinite power of coincidence—synchrodestiny. The techniques he teaches for this to occur are based on one of the world's most ancient wisdom traditions—Vedanta. In Sanskrit, the word *veda* means knowledge, and Vedanta is the end (or peak) of all knowledge.

Consciousness is the ultimate reality, and the nonlocal ground of being is what differentiates into an objective and subjective reality. The subjective reality is our thoughts, feelings, emotions, aspirations, memories, and desires. The objective reality is the world that we experience through our senses. Objective and subjective reality are independent but also acausally related to each other. The inner and outer worlds are a part of a single and unified intelligence and field of activity. The outer world mirrors who we are in a given point in space.

Your life reflects the state of your consciousness, and the state of the world reflects the state of the collective consciousness. At any

HEALING THE MODERN WORLD TRANCE

given time, your reality is orchestrated by your sense of self. If your sense of self is constricted, you will most likely have a constricted view of the environment. If your sense of self is expanded, you will be open to the intentions that are fulfilling themselves in the physical environment as synchronicity. Your expanded self feels peaceful, free, and unbounded. Your constricted self feels greedy, aggressive, arrogant, and unhappy. At the macro level, a culture that has a constricted identity will focus on profit-making, unfair competition, economic imperialism, military conflict, nationalism, and fear.[cxxi] A critical mass of people expressing their expanded selves to fulfill their personal desires could, in turn, change the entire system upon which a society is built. Such a transformed culture would be based more on service, sharing, and compassion rather than greed and competition. In a society in which we could aspire to the expression of our highest selves, we would see that love is the force that is the beating heart of the universe.

The image you see reflects multiples of six-sided geometry. It represents the space–power–time that is transmuted by consciousness. The Hopi tradition views the quantum concept of time and space as holographic rather than linear, like a river on which one can travel forward and backwards. All events have more than one possible outcome. Quantum physics refers to this as the observer affecting the outcome of the experiment. On a metaphysical level, it refers to the ability to manifest our intentions into future outcomes. Whichever way you decide to view this ancient concept, this wisdom lies in the fact that we, as individuals, have an effect on the holographic nature of reality. When you take responsibility for the consequences of your behavior and your thoughts, you learn how to use the power of intention. By transmuting a fear-based model of thinking, we are helping to bring forth unity consciousness.

IV. WHERE DO WE GO FROM HERE?

This is how the compassionate universe works: we enrich ourselves by enriching nature; nature enriches herself by enriching us

—Eknath Easwaran

As you look to the future, think about the metamorphosis of the caterpillar into a butterfly. When a caterpillar reaches a certain point in its evolution, it becomes voracious. At the same time, imaginal cells wake up, vibrating at a different frequency from the other cells, and the caterpillar turns into a sort of nutritive soup. This contains the caterpillar's genetic future, and as the old cells dissolve and separate, they orchestrate into a completely new being. We are the imaginal cells of the universe. We need to have a change in consciousness and commitment for the privilege we have of undertaking this challenge. Like the imaginal cells, we must cluster and work together to create a sustainable future.

Designing a system that would lead to sustainable prosperity is an epic challenge. A new model must lead to greater security, open government, and open business practices. Changing the world is a huge growth opportunity and a necessary task that we must undertake for the future generations. This is a moment of creative innovation in a way we've never seen before. Millions of people are coming together to invent tools, models, and ideas that will make the world better. Our fate lies in the innovative ability to find new ideas and solutions. We each have a part to play. We need as many people as possible who are thinking for themselves and sharing what they know. We need people who can create their own versions of the pieces of the puzzle that come together. We need individual action that will influence others. When we jump on the chance to make changes that speak to the people, we meaningfully express who we are. The world needs people who are deeply engaged with the business of designing their lives in a way that not only speaks to them but to the world as well.

We're living beyond our ecological means and are overtaxing the world in ways that will require our children to be the ones to clean up after our mess. We here in the developed world are using more than our required share and are setting up models and paradigms that are leading the way toward more unsustainability. You can make the world a place where you want to live, knowing that the money can flow in for you to use as a resource to direct it in ways that benefit our world. Paul Hawken talks about how remaining awake and engaged in creating a new vision for the future means being in a state of *blessed unrest*. This is where we are fully aware of where we are, yet we are also able to see a future of where we wish to go. We create possibilities toward that future and are compelled to get out and do things. We allow ourselves to become instruments of a higher intelligence working through us. This is the moment when the human species can rise to its full potential. We have created for ourselves the greatest challenge we can ever face, and this activates our potential to realize the most meaningful lives we could ever live.

We are powerful as individuals, but the planet is in peril, and we need each other to create a new and great future for our planet. Planning for sustainability is like planning for retirement. We save money and build up an investment portfolio. As we get older, we try to live off the revenue created by our portfolios. The capital we have been given in terms of our natural resources is something that should be used in a way that ensures that untouched revenue is available for the future. Ideally, we should be leaving the capital alone completely and living off its interest. What happens if our bills are higher than the amount our interest is paying out? We start spending capital, and in the next year, we're working with less capital and less interest. If our bills continue to increase, we continue to dip into our capital and have less interest. If this continued, we would spiral into bankruptcy. The actual approximation of how long it will take us to fall into this type of bankruptcy is twenty-five years from now. If we don't stop mowing through our natural capital by 2030, we may not even have enough left to forge through to a different path. This is why the present moment is so crucial. If we don't make a commitment to profoundly change the impact we are making on the planet by 2050, we're probably headed for catastrophe. This isn't to cause fear in anyone, but simply to remind ourselves that creating a new model must be accomplished in our lifetime.

We need a new model that allows prosperity in a sustainable manner. This new model will allow people the opportunities to make a profit, keep a profit, and simultaneously heal the planet's ecosystem. This isn't easy in a world in which over 2 billion people have no access to electricity and no safe methods of disposing of their sewage. In fact, it's an epic challenge in a world in which more than a billion people drink fetid water, don't have enough to eat, or are one bad harvest away from mass starvation. According to economists, between $64 billion and $128 billion is lost annually from the developing world because of malnutrition. Education is on the decline. Out of approximately 875 million people in the world who are illiterate, 60% of them are women. For the poorest 1 billion in the world, life is an inescapable trap. For the neighboring 2 billion, life is only slightly better, yet it creates an instability that makes it difficult to progress.[cxxii]

The environment indeed unravels in this context. Large chunks of the world are full of corruption, where debt is strangling many developing countries and has them indebted to developed-world banks. Chaos and corruption make this work more difficult, but this is no excuse. In the next twenty-five years, we *need* to redesign the fabric of our civilization. The model we replace it with must be more sustainable. It must offer everyone the chance of prosperity and the opportunity to transform chaos and corruption. Change takes time, and unfortunately, we don't have very much of it. Even if we agreed as a species today to completely change our ways, we would still have to change our technologies and practices to set up a new system.

Not only do we have to come up with an answer that gives us a smaller pool of capital to allow for change to take effect, we also need to aim to live in a way that has less impact on the planet. We will need to retool, redesign, and initially expend a lot of resources to rebuild systems. We're already running on a deficit that is growing, and we don't have the time to "try something out" and hope for the best. Once we have unraveled the fabric of our planet, it will never come back to us. We must move to a new standard of sustainability—one that is even higher than our current standards—while providing opportunities for prosperity to billions of people in the world. We *need* to do this in the next twenty-five years.

This is where *you* come in. You are an integral part of this change. This is where you can realize that doing the right thing in an intelligent way can also pay well. Become aware of how you are living your life. If you saved energy, you'd also save money. If you lived in a close-knit community and cut down your commute, you'd also have more time to spend with family and friends. You can take your money and invest it into a company that's doing something smart. The world is full of growth opportunities. Fortunes can be made by those who invest in clean energy and new technology, and a ton of money will be saved by those who green their lives, homes, cities, and infrastructures.

In the age of technology, we are in a moment of time in which we can innovate with people from all over the world, exchanging ideas for world-changing models. This is a revolution of people who are committed to playing their part in solving problems. What's needed is for millions of us to wake up, think for ourselves, and share what we know. Every person has something to contribute, whether it's a skill, an experience, or privilege. When we take the opportunity to make changes that are important to us, we also express who we are. This is the one moment in which you need *not* follow another person's instructions on how to design your better life. The world needs passionate people who are deeply engaged in the process of designing their lives in a way that speaks truthfully to them.

CHAPTER 4

Work and Wellness

The symbol of the butterfly speaks of transformation. It is time to open ourselves to the wisdom that is coming our way through rational and intuitive sources. Quantum physics tells us that tiny packets of light comprise all the matter in the universe. Between these packets of light are "choice points," which we always have the opportunity to choose. Open up to the shifting paradigm of our world and allow this transformation to become a joyful acceptance of the dance of life.

The Changing World Paradigm

Environmental activist Paul Hawken wrote an article in 2007 for *Orion* magazine called "To Remake the World: Something Earth-changing is Afoot Among Civil Society." At that time, he talked about how he believed there were between one and two million organizations working toward ecological sustainability and social justice in the world. He spent years researching this phenomenon, created a global database of these organizations (wiser.org), and came to the conclusion that this was the largest social movement of our civilization.

The movement he described has three basic roots: environmental and social justice movements, as well as indigenous cultures' resistance to globalization. This worldwide phenomenon consists of research institutes, community development agencies, village- and citizen-based organizations, corporations, networks, faith-based groups, trusts, and foundations. Hawken himself has said, "Describing the breadth of the movement is like trying to hold the ocean in your hand. It is that large."[cxxiii] Furthermore, he describes this movement as, "nonviolent, and grassroots...it shares a basic set of fundamental understandings about the Earth, how it functions, and the necessity of fairness and equity for all people partaking of the planet's life-giving systems."[cxxiv]

This is a movement that brings about ideas for solving what appear to be insoluble global dilemmas, such as poverty, climate change, terrorism, ecological degradation, polarization of income, and loss of culture. It isn't trying to save the world, but is instead working to transform it. Transformation, not salvation, is key. Hawken gives us a deep sense of hope that this movement will prevail because we find within it humanity's willingness to restore, reform, recover, and reconsider life itself. This process of healing is a tremendously sacred act in which we are all connected.

The entrepreneurs of our time have just as much of a role to play in this movement as do the activists, volunteers, and community organizers. These nouveau entrepreneurs are the people out there creating a revolutionized system of business and work. One of my favorite mentors in this field is Marie Forleo. As creator of her own socially conscious empire, she's a mentor to people all over the world who are redefining what it means to make a living. Being rich is also about unlocking spiritual potential, nurturing health and happiness, and tapping into unique talents that make a difference in the world. Entrepreneurialism today is becoming more about changing the world and having time to do the things you love. This revolution is paving the way for a sustainable business movement.

On a deeper level, fulfilling your purpose is also about tapping into the "why" of your being. In the book *Start with Why*, Simon Sinek talks about how easy it is for a business to explain what it does and how it does what it does, but very few businesses can articulate *why* they do what they do. The *why* isn't based on money or profit or quality products and services. These are results. The *why* is more personal. It's about asking why a business exists and why people should care. Knowing the why refines strategy, branding, marketing, products, and services. Sinek describes how before gaining power or achieving impact, an arrow must be pulled backward *away* from the target. This is where the why becomes a process of discovery and where it derives its power.

Our why is often based on feelings that are controlled by the part of the brain that has no capacity for language. This is the reason putting our feelings into words is sometimes so difficult. We can know that something "feels right" but not necessarily know how to articulate it in words. We have to first discover and articulate the why before knowing the direction of our internal compass, which will become the driving force that guides everything we do.[cxxv] This world would be a much happier place if people spent more time articulating why they do what they do.

The Work and Wellness Paradigm

The world is changing as you read this. Today, industries are being reinvented, and people are choosing to take back their freedom, health, and power. In the book *Choose Yourself*, James Altucher talks about this trend and says, "New tools and economic forces have emerged to make it possible for individuals to create art, make millions of dollars and change the world without 'help.' Opportunities are rising out of the ashes of the broken system to generate real inward success (personal happiness and health) and outward success (fulfilling work and wealth).[cxxvi]"

THE SACRED PATH OF ECO-CONSCIOUSNESS

Indeed, this is a trend we're going to continue to watch unfold. President Obama himself has said that, "Globalization and technology has robotized 'entire occupations' like bank tellers and travel agents."[cxxvii] With the advent of technology, jobs held by humans will be increasingly replaced by robots. After all, we don't need to give robots health insurance or overtime. We see how the traditional paths of lifetime employment with a company is one of days past because independent consultants and freelancers are cheaper than full-time employees with benefits. Certain professions are being outsourced overseas, where costs are a fraction of what they are in the US. The concept of job security is not what it once was.

According to an infographic by San Francisco-based startup Funders and Founders, by 2030, robots will be able to perform most manual labor, replacing actual human labor.[cxxviii] By 2030, other non-manual labor jobs will most likely be held by independent contractors comprising consultants, freelancers, and contractors. These contractors cost companies 30% less, require no benefits, no supervision, and are "pay as you go." The majority of specialized jobs will be outsourced to countries where people are willing to do the same work for a fraction of the cost. We see this trend unfolding throughout the world. Today, in South Korea, the human workforce is slowly being replaced; there are 347 robots per 10,000 employees.[cxxix]

What will the job market look like in about fifteen years? According to some, you will probably first see the tribe of *sidepreneurs*, who will be doing the creative jobs independently here and there. This tribe of smaller business entrepreneurs will be the jack-of-all-trades in our world, able to multitask with jobs that range from programming, design, and marketing to sales. The world of marketing changes exponentially each month. Marketers today are creative writers and experts of human psychology, and they have a deep understanding of the ins and outs of e-mail marketing, tracking, measuring tools, analytics, trends, and content development.

With this changing business climate, more people are realizing that they value the freedom that comes along with working on their own terms. People are leaving their nine-to-five jobs to pursue a passion. It's a revolution known as the "rise of the creative class" or "the freelance economy." According to the Office of National Statistics, approximately 14 out of 100 workers in the United States last year were self-employed.[cxxx] From 2000 to 2011, the number of small-scale entrepreneurs grew by 10.7 million. On the other end of the spectrum, total wage and salary employment grew by only 105,000 during that same period. According to the Bureau of Economic Analysis of the United States Department of Commerce data, 99% of the total increase in employment from 2000 to 2011 was in the self-employed category. During the period from 2007 to 2011, a time known as the Great Malaise, the number of entrepreneurs continued to grow, although this was a time of recession.[cxxxi]

One of the biggest turning points in the rise of micro-entrepreneurialism has been technology. The rise of this new economy is built on the empowerment of individuals. We are creating our own jobs and shifting our perspectives of life, time, and money. Technology has provided us a means to work from anywhere in the world. Professionals of all walks of life are flocking to this lifestyle because it grants them more time with families, greater flexibility, and a higher quality of life. The ability to focus on our family, health, and self-care depends on having more time and a more flexible schedule. The path of becoming a conscious entrepreneur is one of value creation, where the exciting opportunity to take risks also brings along the exciting opportunities to make life better for all.

The Disappearing American Dream

More and more entrepreneurs today are doing the things they love while being visionaries in the process. The goods and services they offer are often molded from the fabric of authenticity, uniqueness of experience, and personal attention. A large percentage of these entrepreneurs value the importance of running responsible commerce, and often the money that goes into purchasing from them also goes into the support of local communities, with sustainable commitments. This new freedom economy works because it is good for economic growth and leads to better lives. Technology allows greater autonomy, flexibility, and a more human infrastructure. Life is, after all, how you spend your time.

Today, the American dream as we know it is disappearing, and a new paradigm is emerging. Back in the day, the American dream was nothing more than a marketing slogan created by Fannie Mae to persuade people to start taking mortgages. The American dream forced us into believing we needed to buy a bigger home, have two cars instead of one, and send all our children to college. Today, the American dream isn't possible unless a home has a double income and children rushing from one place to the next. The American dream is paying other people to raise our children while we spend our free time wrapped up in consumerism, addictions to social media, TV, food, alcohol, drugs, or even going to the gym. Within the American dream, we are bombarded with an overstimulation of music, movies, media, and information. Today, the rules of the old world are quickly dissolving, and as some people desperately attempt to hold on, others are jumping on the fast-moving bandwagon. The American dream is dying. We are becoming aware that the ideal is no longer to have two big houses, three cars, bills, debt, two full-time jobs, and more toys than anyone needs.

The Supermom Syndrome

Becoming a mother gave me the push to contribute my gifts in a way that supports the vision for the type of world I want my son to grow up in. We here in the modern world sacrifice our health and time with our family to have a career. We've been programmed to believe that we have to have a certain type of house, mortgage, car, and education for our children. Dual incomes are a requirement just to keep up, and we make ourselves sick in the process. Katrina Alcorn, author of *Maxed Out: American Mom on the Brink*, talks about her experience as a smart, successful working mom. In describing her own experience, she says, "On the surface, I was doing everything that I was supposed to be doing and it looked like everything was fine. But inside, I was just falling apart. I was having a lot of anxiety and insomnia and there was all this stress. There was too much on my plate. I lost my appetite, I was getting depressed." On the way to Target to buy diapers one day, she had a breakdown. She ended up quitting her job and trying to make sense of what happened.[cxxxii]

Alcorn writes about how most jobs in the United States are still made for people who have an adult at home who can take care of the kids, do the grocery shopping, fill out the school forms, and attend the parent-teacher conferences in the middle of the day. Many working women are on the brink of this dysfunction in a society that expects them to be able to do things they don't have time to do anymore.

Women push themselves, trying to make it all work, and often make themselves sick. Of the countries in the developed world, the United States has some of the worst policies related to supporting working families. It is one of the few countries in the world that do not provide paid parental leave for new parents and do not guarantee paid sick time. The world culture also encourages some of the longest hours of any workers in any developed country. Alcorn talks about the unspoken rule as a professional: "You don't take time off, you never unplug and you're always available nights and weekends."[cxxxiii] Alcorn, now self-employed, considers herself the "best boss she ever had."

A study released by CareerBuilder found that nearly 1 in 3 (30%) of women who have had a child in the past three years have cut short their maternity leaves, not taking as much as their employers' policies allow. Of women who have had children in the past three years, fewer than half (44%) took eight weeks or more of maternity leave. The rest took less—often far less. According to the survey, 12% of women went back to work after taking leave of only two weeks or less.[cxxxiv] Other studies have shown similar findings. After California passed a state law requiring paid maternity leave to workers, a 2011 study found that only one-third of female workers were taking full advantage of their leave. The reason: They feared doing so would make their employers "unhappy" and possibly result in them being fired.[cxxxv]

There's a story of how, in 2012, a federal judge ordered a *Milwaukee medical staffing company to pay $148,000 to* a former bookkeeper for the firm after the company fired her while she was on maternity leave.[cxxxvi] The judge found that the owner of the company had referred to her pregnancy as a joke, insisting that the maternity leave should only last a few days, and then fired her while she was still in the hospital recuperating from a Caesarean birth. Shockingly, statistics suggest that *pregnancy discrimination remains a pervasive problem.*[cxxxvii] The Equal Employment Opportunity Commission received 5,800 pregnancy-related discrimination complaints in 2011, up from 4,000 in 1997.

The prospects for guaranteed paid maternity leave are diminishing in the United States. The Families and Medical Leave Act, passed in 1993, guarantees most workers the right to take three months *unpaid leave.*[cxxxviii] The US is joined by just three other countries (Swaziland, Liberia, and Papua New Guinea) on the list of countries that do not guarantee paid maternity leave. The number of American employers offering fully paid leave is dropping, according to the Families and Work Institute. In 2005, of the employers who provided paid leave, 17% offered full pay. In 2011, that figure dropped to 9%.

Never in our collective lifetimes has it been so important to take a stand toward a new paradigm. It's happening as you read this. Baby boomers are recreating their careers, and the younger millennials are rejecting the traditional career path to find work that's more meaningful. There's a collective flow of fresh ideas, new ways of thinking, and the ability to make things happen. People are beginning to set up shop in random places; you don't even have to be in an entrepreneurial city or place anymore. With the advent of social media, there seems no end to the marketing opportunities available to people nowadays. This is truly a unique moment in our history.

Intentions for a New Economy

It's my hope that, after reading this book, you will walk away with even the tiniest spark that will light your fire. The time has come for you to begin expressing your creativity. It's time to align your purpose with the prosperity you deserve. You're ready to let go of all those things that have stood in the way of making this commitment to yourself in the past. Value systems are changing, and I am seeing people become increasingly aware of the unsustainability of our old systems. Younger generations are beginning to realize that the old system is broken. This system no longer holds the answer to our dreams and desires nor is it necessarily sustainable. *Bigger, better, and faster* things are plunging the world into further despair. Business *as usual* is no longer an option.

Our economic system is sick and in need of renewal. Humanity is desperately in need of a transition. A few generations ago, we looked up to growth, the conquest of nature, and the expansion of the human realm as integral. Today, people's values are increasingly changing, and we are realizing our need to create a world that's more sustainable, fulfilling, and socially just. The energy behind how we prosper and make money needs to come into alignment with our highest values.

Furthermore, people are realizing that the traditional roadways to education and a career won't be sustainable for future generations. As a parent, you have genuine hopes for the education you'll be able to provide for your children, but even that is becoming an unsustainable goal. Statistics show us that, today, two out of three people borrow money to pay for college and that tuition is increasing at a rate of 5% to 7% a year.

Today, approximately 13% of students default on student loans within three years of their graduation. What causes this default? The inability to keep up with payments triggers interest rates that blow up into amounts far more than were initially borrowed. This has turned into a society in which we want our children to study hard, get good grades, be ambitious, and achieve their dreams, but at the expense of turning education (a public good) into a privately financed investment.

Industries are changing so rapidly that somehow is doesn't make as much sense to spend so much on a college education when opportunities to do something big are presented to us everywhere. I don't believe that, collectively, this *debt of degrees* can go on. Parents saving for their child's education in the United States will have to have approximately $360,000 to finance a four-year degree fifteen years down the road. So many people put themselves into debt when they don't even know if they want to make a life out of what they're studying. However, the reality is that even education is quickly changing. Fifteen to twenty years from now, the advances in digitally mediated, self-organized, and experiential learning will emerge into higher-quality options with lower-cost alternatives for our children. Down the road, there will be more worldwide opportunities and equality for advances in education. The tools to which we have access today make it possible for us to create a new system and change the world. We need change to ripple through the industries of art, design, engineering, science, and biology. We need to create a new generation of what we consider to be "stuff." This is the stuff that uses minimal energy, nontoxic chemicals, is recyclable, and isn't harmful to nature.

Aligning with your purpose means that you're also holding strong intentions behind your actions and goals. Anyone can become a game changer, and more people are choosing to do so every day. All you have to do is take a look at the *Forbes* list of entrepreneurs under the age of thirty who are making a difference, and you'll see the powerful energy behind our youth.[cxxxix] Take the Global Poverty Project, whose cofounder, Hugh Evans, set an intention to end extreme poverty (which equates to living on less than $1.25 a day). Evans used social media to launch awareness campaigns, encouraged people to take online actions (like tweeting about poverty or watching an educational video on YouTube) in exchange for points that could be redeemed for tickets to those campaign events. The twenty-three-year old founder of Buena Nota started an organization that informs, educates, and connects Colombians with regard to social problems and their solutions. Buena Nota has managed to bring together more than one million actively involved individuals. This has paved the way for the creation of a Social Entrepreneurship Bank to connect ventures with investors.[cxl] I could go on and on about our incredible youth doing inspiring things to make a difference.

WORK AND WELLNESS

Whatever you uniquely choose to create is a living entity that you are birthing into the world. The process is an incredibly sacred act that demands your authenticity, integrity, and respect. You are the one bringing your vision alive. The more in line with your truth you are, the more authenticity you hold and the more you adhere to your highest values and ideals. I want you to create a life that not only expresses who you are but also brings you fulfillment in every aspect of your life. When you tap into the authentic vision of your spirit, magic unfolds. You motivate and inspire others, you attract the right types of people, you stimulate the emergence of new ideas, and you make the world a happier place. This next part of the book focuses on your commitment to self-care. It is where the real work begins before we can extend it into the realms of what I have been talking about here in the outer world.

CHAPTER 5

Love, Gratitude, Forgiveness

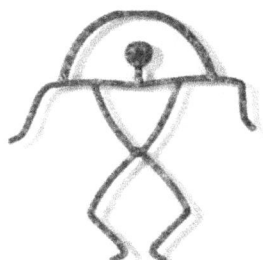

While visiting Maui, my husband, son, and I took a hike through the Sacred Iao Valley. We decided to take *the road less traveled* and jumped beyond a "No Trespassing" sign into an area of forest that we felt called to follow. That sensation urged us to walk in a certain direction until we stumbled across a rock. This rock was evidently a sacred spot as it was surrounded by offerings. Engraved on the rock was an ancient Hawaiian petroglyph of the Rainbow Man (as seen in the symbol above).

The rainbow is the celestial path that the Hawaiian gods used to come down to earth from the cloud islands. The Rainbow Goddess, *Anuenue*, who is sister to the primal gods *Kane* and *Kanaloa*, acts as a messenger of the gods. *Lono*, the God of Fertility and Music, descended on a rainbow to marry *Laka*, the Hawaiian Goddess of Music and Dance. The rainbow is the pathway that the souls of the dead take to travel to the heavenly realms. The souls walk on the rainbow path to pass through *Kuaihelani*, a mysterious floating island whose name means to "support the heavens or spiritual" in reaching the sacred land of *Nu'umealani* (the fragrant land of the heavenly one). The rainbow is also a symbol of transformation, signifying those who travel freely between the upper and lower worlds, living like gods among humans. Featured as a pathway between dimensions in Hawaiian mythology (also seen in various cultures around the world), it also acts as a footstool for *Malanai-kuaheahea*, the wife of the legendary transpacific voyager and astronomer whose name, *Maliki'i*, is also the Hawaiian term for the Pleiades star cluster from which the first Hawaiians came to earth.

Often found among Hawaiian petroglyphs are the depictions of a rainbow warrior. The rainbow man petroglyph has been interpreted to mean *Keeper of the Aina* (keeper of the land). When you examine the petroglyph found in the sacred Iao Valley on Maui, you can see that the arc or rainbow begins and rests on his shoulders, suggesting man's responsibility to earth as a rainbow warrior. He was one who revered the ancient wisdom found in the world's cultures, actively taking action for peace, harmony, and enlightenment of the community.[cxli] There is a saying in Hawaiian, "E Mau Ke Ea I Ka 'Aina I Ka Pono," which means, "The very life of the land and all that nourishes life is protected by the right intentions, the right actions, and the right outcomes of the people.[cxlii]"

Gandhi once said, "Our greatness lies not so much in being able to remake the world as being able to remake ourselves[cxliii]." In this chapter, I share the legends of the land of my birth. There are timeless lessons to be found amongst these legends, and this is important in supporting the merging of the old with the new. The Hawaiians have long known of the interconnectedness between all things. It is only recently that scientists are beginning to understand how deeply we are connected at an intimate level. Take the theory of "entanglement," which Einstein has famously described as "spooky action from a distance."[cxliv] This entanglement can be seen as a sort of "voodoo reality." The point at which you can directly affect things that are right next to you is referred to as *locality*. Voodoo reality contradicts locality because it involves doing something in one place and affecting something in another without the need for travel. This may not sound plausible to some, and even Einstein himself said it was *spooky*.

Both theoretical and experimental considerations support the conclusion that the universe admits interconnections that are not local. A class of experiments performed during the last couple of decades has indeed shown that something we do over here (such as measuring certain properties of a particle) can be subtly entwined with something that happens over there (such as the outcome of measuring certain properties of another distant particle) without anything being sent from here to there[cxlv] and even if there isn't enough time for light to travel between the events. Intervening space does not ensure that two objects are separate since quantum mechanics allows an entanglement to exist between them. According to quantum theory, the quantum connection between two particles can persist even if they are on opposite sides of the universe. From the standpoint of entanglement, there may be trillions of miles of space between two points that seem like they are next to each other.[cxlvi]

The Lakota are onto this concept of entanglement when they say, "Mitakuye Oyasin" (meaning "All My Relations"). Even before the advent of quantum physics, they had an inner knowledge of the interconnectedness of all things. Take, for instance, the Global Consciousness Project. This organization has been gathering data continuously from a global network of physical random number generators located in 70 host sites around the world. The data are then transmitted to a central archive, which now contains more than 12 years of random data in parallel sequences of synchronized 200-bit trials every second.[cxlvii] The purpose of this experiment is to examine subtle correlations that reflect the presence and activity of consciousness in the world. The results show that when emotional, large world events occur (massive earthquakes, terrorist attacks, the Olympic opening ceremonies) where millions of people are tuned in to similar emotions and intentions, these random data machines become more "coherent," straying from their random output.[cxlviii] On some level, a collective intention—the focused conscious experience of millions of people—ripples through the fabric of our realities.

THE SACRED PATH OF ECO-CONSCIOUSNESS

In Hawai'i, there is a philosophy of Aloha 'Aina, meaning "to love that which nourishes you." The land and the environment give us what we need to sustain ourselves. The Hawaiians believe in self-mastery—knowing how to survive and to self-correct. Rima Morrell, author of *The Sacred Power of Huna*, beautifully describes the concept of Aloha 'Aina and our interconnectedness when she writes, "The keys to being able to 'make magic' are to be aware of our interconnectedness with the substance of all and to generate power by focusing the great light of our being. The free-floating silver pieces of aka, the stuff of which the universe is made, do not possess mana in themselves. They are like a circuit whose electrical current hasn't been switched on; in fact, the lines of the circuit first have to be connected by the practitioner. ... It is possible for all of us to transform our aka into akua [the gods and goddesses of huna] if we learn how to activate our consciousness. ... That's why creativity is so important. ... Creativity is how we liberate ourselves from our habitual structures and familiar choices.[cxlix]"

Hawaiian folklore tells of the three piko, where the piko at the top of our heads connects us with our ancestors and the cosmos, the abdomen piko connects us to our families and the earth, and the genital piko connects us to creation (which is our children, the future, and the generations to come). This *kulueana*, or responsibility, is not only for the present, but also for the past and future in one space–time continuum. Thousands of years ago, people told stories, which offered knowledge and guidance through genuine connection. This is what connects and unites us. All indigenous peoples understand this. Hawaiian chants talk about creation, the beginning of life, swirling, and the movement of the universe. This interrelated connection to all is an electromagnetic field of life around our entire planet and brings healing to the alienation, contamination, destruction, greed, pollution, and poverty that have been created by destroying our earth. This nature is within each one of us.

The Hawaiians talk about how their ancestors came here from the stars tens of thousands of years ago. They brought with them a sacred wisdom called *Ho'ala Huna* (meaning "that which causes an awakening to the secret or sacred awareness of reality"). This knowledge was said to be the science of the world of spirit and form. It was kept within a special priesthood lineage known as the *Mo'o* or "dragon priests." It is said that these priests used this knowledge to build a powerful culture in a land called *Mu*, which then later spread to Egypt and regions of Central and South America. This motherland was destroyed during a battle. To preserve elements of this sacred knowledge, the priests (who were its keepers in Egypt) migrated eastward across northern India and southern Asia. Their goal was to reach a land in the middle of the ocean where the knowledge could be preserved. As they migrated eastward, they founded learning centers, which are thought to have become the starting points of many of the world's religions. They eventually arrived in Hawai'i sometime before 600 BC.[cl]

Throughout pre-ali'i Polynesia (750 BC to 1,250 AD), Ho'ala Huna resulted in a civilization so advanced that it is said that its people lived in a paradise. People thrived in complete peace and harmony for almost 2,000 years. Its system of conflict resolution and justice was a model of effectiveness. Families exemplified the ideals of safety and nurturing and produced people who were deeply in tune with their higher body, mind, and spirit. Life was seen as a divine opportunity to develop one's spirit. In learning how to master their spirits, people learned how to master the flow of life energy. By learning how to master the flow of life energy, they learned how to master their divine ability to create. They were a people who took responsibility for how they created their lives. The teachings of Ho'ala Huna are firmly rooted in one of universal truth. It teaches that enlightenment is the purpose of life, expanding consciousness is the nature of divinity, and that the attainment of total consciousness is the nature of Godhood, which is the purpose of every conscious being.[cli] *Huna* is the ancient knowledge that enables a person to connect to his or her highest wisdom within. Huna teacher, Serge Kalihi King, articulated the seven principles of Huna in the following way:[clii]

1 **Ike**: The world is what you think it is.
2 **Kala**: There are no limits, and everything is possible.
3 **Makia**: Energy flows where attention goes.

THE SACRED PATH OF ECO-CONSCIOUSNESS

4 **Manawa**: Now is the moment of power.
5 **Aloha:** To love is to be happy with.
6 **Mana**: All power comes from within.
7 **Pono:** Effectiveness is the measure of truth.

If one delves further into the teachings of Huna, one learns that the ancient Kahunas of Hawai'i viewed feelings of guilt as the leading cause of illness in the mental, emotional, and physical bodies. They believed in healing guilt through an ancient process, found within Huna, known as *Ho'oponopono*. This is an old practice of reconciliation—of "making right." This is the belief that through the healing of self, one heals the world. Ho'oponopono is the process of making things right with the people we carry in our lives. In this practice, we clean our relationships with others. You may have heard the story of Dr. Stanley Hew Len. About thirty years ago, there was a clinic for mentally ill criminals at the Hawai'i State Hospital. A nurse who worked there during those years described it as a place so dark that not even paint would stick to the walls. Aggression between the inmates and staff members proliferated through this clinic. Because of this sense of violence and terror, the inmates were seldom allowed outside. Staff turnover was also high.

One day, the clinic appointed a new clinical psychologist by the name of Dr. Stanley Hew Len. At first, it didn't seem as if he was doing anything in particular. He was exceptionally relaxed and cheerful. Occasionally, he would ask for inmate files. The interesting thing was that he never actually tried to see any of them personally. Instead, he sat in his office and looked at their files. Even more interesting was that, little by little, things started to change at the hospital. The clinic was looking cleaner, and more and more inmates were being allowed outside without causing trouble to the staff. There were noticeably positive changes occurring among the prisoners, and they were significant enough to slowly release them one by one back into society. Dr. Hew Len worked at this clinic for almost four years. By the time he left, only a couple of inmates remained, and they were relocated so that the clinic could close its doors.

LOVE, GRATITUDE, FORGIVENESS

So, what happened? Dr. Hew Len never personally interacted with the inmates. He explained that what he did was work on healing himself, using the ancient process of Ho'oponopono. Of this process, he said, "I was simply healing the part of me that created them." He sat in his office, looking at patient files. While looking at them, he would allow himself to feel something in relation to them, such as pain or empathy. Through this, he would begin the process of healing himself by taking full responsibility for what was going on with a given patient.

Ho'oponopono is based on the knowledge that anything that happens to you (or anything that you perceive) is your own creation and responsibility. The world is your creation. Taking responsibility doesn't mean that you are to blame for everything; it means that you are responsible for healing yourself so that you may heal whatever or whoever it is that appears to you as a problem. The most common (and simplified) version of Ho'oponopono involves four steps.

Step 1: Repentance (saying, "I'm sorry.") This step puts you in a position of taking responsibility for the problems in your life. You can do this by saying, "I am aware that I am responsible for <issue> in my life, and I'm sorry that something in my consciousness has caused this."

Step 2: Forgiveness (saying, "Please forgive me.") In this step, you ask for forgiveness. Think about what you feel from step 1, and ask to be forgiven. You can do this over and over again, and it can be about anything and anyone.

Step 3: Gratitude (saying, "Thank you.") In this step, you are feeling gratitude. You can thank anything or anyone. You can thank yourself for being you or thank your body for working so hard. Keep feeling grateful, and keep saying thank you.

Step 4: Love (saying, "I love you.") There is nothing as powerful as love. Again, you can say this to anyone or anything. Love yourself, your body, your home, your car, your family, and even your enemies.[cliii] The four steps in Ho'oponopono allow us to take full responsibility for ourselves. By following these steps, we clear and release the negative energies associated with a person or thing causing us pain, and we do so using love, forgiveness, and gratitude. As the writer Joe Vitale once said, "Ho'oponopono impacts the Akashic record on the collective soul level of all thoughts, feelings, and actions humans have ever made since the first moment of creation."[cliv]

These mythological stories instruct us to allow our *Kāne* (higher selves) to burst forth. The gods and goddesses each teach us different things. For example, *Poli'ahu* (the Goddess of the Snow) teaches us the value of well-placed emotion. *Hina* (the Goddess of the Moon) shows us how to increase our focused consciousness. The home of Poli'ahu is located on Mauna Kea, on the Big Island of Hawai'i. Mauna Kea, one of the island's most sacred peaks, is also called the "mountain of clarity."[clv] It is said that Poli'ahu found her home near the summit, with hair of icicles hanging from the rocks. In time past, she would constantly find herself in battles with her sister, *Pele*. Pele would overwhelm the land with fire, and Poli'ahu would retaliate by covering it with snow. Geologically, one can see this in the strange conical shapes of Mauna Kea.

Mauna Kea has not had an eruption for over a thousand years, and Hawaiian folklore has attributed this to Poli'ahu's state of peace. Near the summit of Mauna Kea lies a mysterious lake called *Waiau*, which has no freshwater springs but is never dry. Legend has it that it is eternally fed by the crystalline goddess Poli'ahu. Every aspect of her home is rich with symbolic meaning. Unlike Pele, Poli'ahu no longer feels the need to erupt in passion. The hidden meaning in her name also refers to the "bosom goddess" because she has learned to overcome the waters of emotion and allowed them to flow into Lake Waiau. Poli'ahu's home is located at the highest point of the land of Hawai'i and the highest mountain in the world (when measured from sea level).

In myths, we find the keys to transformation. When we connect ourselves consciously to ancient mythology, we become bringers of that old knowledge of harmony into our current world. In Hawai'i, ancestors gave their light through mythology. This is the rainbow

LOVE, GRATITUDE, FORGIVENESS

light of traditional knowledge illuminating our dark skies. It doesn't matter what race or culture we associate with; we each need to be the bringer of that old knowledge of harmony.

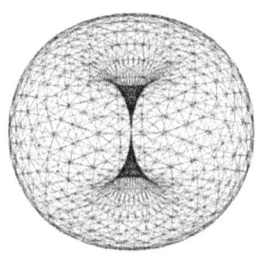

The torus is a piece of sacred geometry. When viewed as three-dimensional, it looks like a donut. This is the primal shape of the universe. It is the simplest geometry of self-referencing. It is a self-organizing system that has the capacity to pull itself together and sustain itself. We see this throughout nature. The human heart has seven muscles that form a torus. The torus also happens to be the shape of the earth's magnetic fields. Like the concept of Ho'oponopono, the lesson in this symbol is for us to forgive and open up our heart connection to the earth. It teaches us to feel gratitude for everything and everyone in our lives. Studies have concluded that the expression of gratitude can have profound and positive effects on our health, our moods and even the survival of our marriages. Drs. Blaire and Rita Justice (University of Texas Health Science Center) have stated that, "a growing body of research shows that gratitude is truly amazing in its physical and psychosocial benefits[clvi]." Robert Emmons, a psychology professor at the University of California at Davis, has found in his research that those who adopt an "attitude of gratitude" as a permanent state of mind experience many health benefits[clvii].

Gratitude also means that we find a place in nature and reconnect with the energy of the planet on a daily basis. We feel thankful for this wondrous planet that is our home. We allow the energy of our earth mother to nourish us. The time has come for us to open ourselves to forgiveness so that we may feel grateful in the love in which we realize the miracle of life.

CHAPTER 6

Purpose and Wellbeing

This is the true joy in life, the being used for a purpose recognized by yourself as a mighty one; the being a force of nature instead of a feverish selfish clod of ailments and grievances complaining that the world will not devote itself to making you happy.

I am of the opinion that my life belongs to the whole community and as long as I live it is my privilege to do for it whatever I can.

I want to be thoroughly used up when I die, for the harder I work, the more I live.

I rejoice in life for its own sake.

Life is no 'brief candle' to me.

It is sort of a splendid torch which I have a hold of for the moment, and I want to make it burn as brightly as possible before handing it over to future generations.

—GEORGE BERNARD SHAW

THE SACRED PATH OF ECO-CONSCIOUSNESS

The circle is a representation of a beginning with no end. It is full of ever-expanding potential. Stepping into the circle allows you to view the whole of existence from a space of holographic oneness. This is the sacred center of creation where you will find unlimited potential and possibility. This is where you create the intentions that will become your reality. You are guided by the breath of knowing that you are a part of all that is. Stepping into your purpose is your path toward wholeness. This is the moment your creation expresses itself as unity acting within your being. The world needs you. You are a crucial part of the whole.

Every person on this planet has a unique set of gifts and offerings to the world. The world needs people who are consciously aware of who they are and where they want to go. In *Ayurveda*, the expression of your highest purpose in life is known as your *dharma*. This comes from the word *dhri,* which means to "hold up" or support from within. A consciousness of abundance is created when we discover and share our inner reservoir of creativity. When you live your dharma, you are doing what feels most fulfilling to *you* while providing value to everyone affected by your actions. The important thing is that you are taking the time to place attention on the meaning you place on your life and how you desire to live it. Often, we find that settling for something causes us to lose sight of our real purpose in life. In the end, all life is fluid and transitory; the only constant is change.

Kurukshetra is the place where the battle of the *Mahabharata* (the largest epic in all of world literature) took place. The Mahabharata has been called a literature in itself. Embedded in this epic masterpiece is one of the finest mystical documents the world has ever seen: *The Bhagavad Gita*. It has been said that the Gita is an internal dialogue between the ordinary human personality about the meaning of life, and our deepest Self, which is divine. In the Gita, *Krishna* (the representation of the spark of divinity that lies at the core of human personality) repeatedly tells the character Arjuna, "I am the Self in the heart of every creature, Arjuna, and the beginning, middle, and end of their existence."[clviii] This statement also distills the essence of the Upanishads, a handbook of the *Perennial Philosophy* in itself. Aldous Huxley called this the Perennial Philosophy because it has appeared in every age and civilization.

This philosophy can be summarized in three statements: (1) There is an infinite and changeless reality beneath the world of change; (2) this reality lies at the core of every human personality; and (3) the purpose of life is to discover this reality experientially and to realize God (by becoming aware of God's presence within oneself) while here on earth. Eknath Easwaran, who translated the Gita, has said that the Upanishads are like "ecstatic slideshows of mystical experience: vivid, disjointed, stamped with the power of direct personal encounter with the divine."[clix]

The Upanishads delineate three ordinary states of consciousness: waking, dreaming, and dreamless sleep. Beyond these three, the Upanishads say, is the unitive state called "the fourth" (or *turiya*). The dream of waking life—the dream of a separate, physical existence—is called the *maya*. In the Gita, maya is the creative power that makes unity appear as the world of innumerable separate things with name and form. This is the separation that is the basis of the dream of our modern world. Like the concept of awakening from the dream of the modern world, it is when we disidentify ourselves with the conditions of perception in maya that we awaken into a higher knowing in which the unity of life is understood. The discipline that helps us reach this state is called *yoga* (meaning state of union). Yoga, not just being a workout one can experience at the gym, is really the experience of *samadhi*, where the state of *moksha* is that which is beyond illusion, or maya (time, space, and causality). This is the state in which the individual realizes that he/she is the Self and not separate from God.

The Upanishadic discovery is that all things are interconnected because, at its deepest level, creation is indivisible. This oneness bestows a balance on the whole of nature, and any disturbance in one place sends ripples everywhere, trembling until balance is restored. Every thought and act has consequences, which themselves have consequences. Life is an intricate web of interconnection. At the heart of this discourse, one can also summarize it in the Lakota saying "all my relations."

THE SACRED PATH OF ECO-CONSCIOUSNESS

The nature of life is to grow toward a joyous expression of itself. The thrust of evolution is to create increasingly complex systems that are capable of higher levels of awareness. The desire to know the self is deep within each of us. This quest has enthralled us since the dawn of civilization. Each society, each time period, carries with it the stories of the great heroes and heroines who have made the "journey" and become examples for us to follow.

In Mesopotamia, there was the king of Erech, *Gilgamesh*, who left his city to find the plant of immortality that was to be found at the bottom of the Cosmic Sea. In ancient Greece, there was *Odysseus*, who sought his island home of Ithaca, and *Jason*, who searched for the Golden Fleece. The Knights of the Round Table in Arthurian England set out on some of the most sacred missions in a quest for the Holy Grail. These myths differ, yet their message is the same. The journey begins when we are challenged and called to fulfill a fuller life, usually with the promise of a new state of being.

Joseph Campbell famously called this the "Hero's Journey." It describes the typical adventure of the archetype known as *The Hero*, the person who goes out and achieves great deeds on behalf of a group, tribe, or civilization. The hero or heroine accepts this challenge with the implications of transformation and metamorphosis, and he or she crosses that initial threshold that marks the beginning of a journey. Death and rebirth are repeated many times in the process, and there are dangers and trials along the way. Every transformation is a dying of the old and a resurrection into something new. The journey takes courage and perseverance and includes uneasy decisions to be made. Without a strong sense of self, many become tired.

The heroes and heroines take the journey aided by unseen forces. Apotheosis is the final achievement, when the traveler returns and becomes an example to others who are also inspired to follow and complete their quest. These are the heroes and heroines who have become the greatest teachers known to us—the seers, saints, prophets, and spiritual leaders. They have reached wholeness and integrated with the cosmos to become conscious instruments.

Maureen Murdock, a student of Campbell, wrote a book titled *The Heroine's Journey*. In contrast to the hero's journey, which is centered on a more "outward" exploration, the heroine's journey is one of "inner" exploration. Victoria Lynn Schmidt, author of the book *45 Master Characters,* says, "The feminine journey is a journey in which the hero gathers the courage to face death and endure the transformation toward being reborn as a complete being in charge of her own life. Her journey starts by questioning authority, then gaining the courage to stand up for herself, and finally embodying the willingness to go it alone and face her own symbolic death."[clx]

This inward journey is one to which many of us can relate.

The story of the journey begins with the heroine sheltered in her bubble—a world designed to protect her. She's safe but is also shielded from the pain and uncertainty of taking risks that are required for her growth. In this bubble, she is asleep to the world around her and ignorant of the power she has to awaken herself. Deep down, the heroine knows she needs to leave the bubble, but she usually relies on some coping strategy to abide living there. Some of us remain in denial; others become extreme people pleasers or (for the more self-aware) feel depressed yet unable to change. Often, an event occurs in her life that is out of her control and shatters her world. The heroine realizes that the bubble she's lived in feels empty and unrewarding. Schmidt says, "She's pushed toward a fork in the road where she must decide whether to go into the world to actively face her fears, or stay where she is and become a passive victim."[clxi] In this phase, the heroine finally understands that her coping strategies don't work.

What is key at this point is the motivation to change. After motivation comes the choice to change. For anyone who has embarked on a "journey," this is usually the hardest step. Perhaps she feels she will never accomplish her goal, or she meets someone who offers to rebuild the bubble for her. By this point, however, the heroine realizes that rebuilding is no longer worth the effort. She ignores all who try to convince her otherwise, and she finally steps out into the world.

The heroine doesn't know where she's headed, so she gathers all the weapons and tools in her personal arsenal that she thinks will help her on her journey. She says goodbye to her old life and coping strategies, and she proceeds to make her first new ally. Schmidt says,

THE SACRED PATH OF ECO-CONSCIOUSNESS

"Whether she realizes it or not, she has friends who support her." Now that the heroine has made her life-changing decision, she realizes that *things must change*. This is a stage about facing her fears and obstacles. At first, the heroine will try to use the weapons and tools she brought along, but they don't necessarily work. The only way through is by finding the inner strength to confront them. The fears and obstacles that must be faced usually relate to one of the following seven inner turmoils. The symbolism of these turmoils can be seen everywhere in life, all around the world. For example, in the book *Avatar: The Last Airbender*, the obstacles coincide with the chakras Aang must open to awaken to his true power[clxii]:

1. The issue of survival, blocked by fear
2. The issue of pleasure, blocked by guilt
3. The issue of willpower, blocked by shame
4. The issue of giving/receiving love, blocked by grief
5. The issue of truth and communication, blocked by the lies we tell ourselves
6. The issue of insight, blocked by illusion
7. The issue of self-awareness, blocked by earthly attachments

To succeed, the heroine must give up all illusion of control, learn to trust her instincts, and surrender to the descent. She must confront her inner demons. Murdock describes this process as an urgent yearning to reconnect with the feminine (often through the healing of the mother–daughter split). This marks the initiation into the *goddess*. The heroine then heals the wounded masculine within and, in the end, emerges with an integration of both masculine and feminine.

PURPOSE AND WELLBEING

In sacred geometry, the symbol of the labyrinth represents the hero or heroine's path. This is an ancient design found across cultures, some dating back thousands of years. The geometry of the labyrinth combines the circle and spiral into a meandering path of purpose. You have to take the way in to find a way out. This is a metaphor for the spiritual path. The shape allows you to feel a heightened awareness as a tool of spiritual exploration. It moves one into a space of inner knowing and then outward into your truth.

Stories of the journey toward integration and self-awareness are told throughout the world. The famous epic by Persian poet *Farid ud-Din Attar*, *The Conference of the Bird*s, beautifully outlines the journey of the self back toward the self. In the poem, the birds of the world gather to decide who is to become their king, as they have none. The *hoopoe*, the wisest bird of them all, suggests that they must find the legendary *Simorgh*, a mythical Persian bird similar to the Western *phoenix*. The hoopoe leads the birds on this journey, with each representing a human fault (that which prevents man from attaining enlightenment). One by one, the birds give up, each offering an excuse as to why it is unable to endure the journey. In each bird, there is a significance that is relatable to the human condition. For example, the nightingale symbolizes the lover, the parrot is seeking the fountain of immortality (not God), and the peacock symbolizes the "fallen soul" who is in alliance with Satan. Along this journey, the birds must cross seven valleys to find the *Simorgh*. Each valley is represented by *Talab* (or yearning), *Eshq* (love), *Marifat* (gnosis), *Istighnah* (detachment), *Tawheed* (unity of God), *Hayrat* (bewilderment), and *Fuqur and Fana* (selflessness and oblivion in God). Eventually, only thirty birds remain as they finally arrive in the land of Simorgh. Upon arrival, all they see is each other and the reflection of themselves in a lake. There is no sign of the mythical Simorgh.

At its essence, this poem teaches us the Sufi doctrine that we are not separate from the universe. In seeking the Simorgh, the remaining thirty birds realize that it is nothing more than their transcendent totality.

THE SACRED PATH OF ECO-CONSCIOUSNESS

The home we seek is in eternity;
The Truth we seek is like a shoreless sea,
Of which your paradise is but a drop.
This ocean can be yours; why should you stop
Beguiled by dreams of evanescent dew?
The secrets of the sun are yours, but you
Content yourself with motes trapped in its beams.
Turn to what truly lives, reject what seems—
Which matters more, the body or the soul?
Be whole: desire and journey to the Whole.[clxiii]

Whatever your journey is in life, your purpose is your unique reason for being on this planet. It's a way of serving yourself and others. Often, it's the very challenges and experiences that we've had to deal with in our lives that inspire us to fulfill a certain mission. We must first go through the *trenches* before we gain mastery over something. In The Upanishads, the ancient Vedic wisdom states, "You are what your deep, driving desire is. As your desire is, so is your intention. As your intention is, so is your will. As your will is, so is your deed. As your deed is, so is your destiny."[clxiv] Our destiny comes from the deepest level of desire and intention. These are completely intertwined. Intention is how you are going to fulfill a certain need that you have. Whether it is a material goal, a spiritual fulfillment, or a relationship goal, it is the intention you have that will lead you to fulfilling your need. "Find something more important than you are," philosopher Dan Dennett once said in discussing *the secret of happiness*, "and dedicate your life to it." How you arrive at your true calling is an intricate and highly individual dance of discovery.

I think one of the greatest myths of modern times is that our purpose is synonymous with the job we have or the type of work we're doing. For most people, a job is a means to pay the bills rather than a way to live our deepest commitments. Purpose isn't necessarily external. It can be about discovering and nurturing who we truly are, and loving ourselves at the deepest level. If more people lived from the level of their passion, their inspired mission, or their love-fueled hobby, it would be a much happier world. Purpose must first be anchored within or we will find ourselves drifting off again and again. Our purpose may adapt and adjust to the changing tides of life, though in itself, it is unchanging.

For Mahatma Gandhi, dharma (as encapsulated in the Gita) could be summed up in one phrase: *nishkama karma* (selfless action). This is a work that is free from selfish desire. Desireless action is, however, not the ideal. Desire is the fuel of life without which nothing would be achieved. What Gandhi spoke of is a "selfish desire." The Gita teaches that this selfish craving is what makes a person feel separate from the rest of life. Nishkama karma is not simply "good work" (or philanthropic activity). Even work that benefits others involves some ego activity. This is not the work of yoga. Action without selfish motive purifies the mind, and the doer becomes less ego-driven. If one is attached to the results of action, it is difficult to truly enjoy what one does. If things don't work out, people usually cling even more to what they do.

The point of the path of love in the Gita is to transform motivation from "I, I, I" to "thou, thou, thou." In the famous verse of chapter nine, Krishna says, "Whatever you do, make it an offering to me. Do it, that is, not for personal reward but out of love for the Lord, present in every creature."[clxv] The person who achieves the state of actionless action is driven by the Self that acts through him or her.

Social Conditioning

To a certain extent, finding your inner purpose requires you to break free from social conditioning. It requires you to let go of the need for external approval. Conditioning is the set of instructions each of us learned to fit in with society. Our family members, teachers, and peer groups were all part of the socialization process. The long-term effect of this socialization is that we seek external approval and external goals in our lives. If we are to take control of our consciousness and pursue our own goals, it is important for us to break free from social programming. When we mistakenly believe that happiness is obtained by achieving external goals, we miss out on enjoying the present moment of life. Most of us are walking around with a repressed inner vitality because of all the demands and expectations we have to keep up with. In Sanskrit, *alaya vigyan* refers to the house where you throw things you want to do but cannot because of social conditioning. We collect all those things by putting them away in the basement, and they accumulate. Eventually, they go into darkness but continue to influence our behaviors. The feeling of losing your mind comes when you can't keep suppressing things anymore.

Does any of the following conditioning sound familiar?

1. **I want more money**

   Thinking you will be happy when you make more money
   To make more money, one must become a workaholic

2. **I want popularity**

   Once you become a certain somebody, people will like and respect you more
   Feeling pressure to keep up with your outside environment

3. **I want to be liked**

   Taking a certain job to pay for high rates of consumption
   Pursuing a goal because it is expected of you
   Being afraid to speak up or share your ideas

4. **I want power**

   Using others to achieve your goals
   Dominate social interactions
   Judgment of other people's weaknesses and failures

We all are guilty of getting caught in our projections onto the situations and people surrounding us. We don't take responsibility for our expectations and judgments; instead, we attribute them to others. What we see in others often belongs to us. Taking responsibility means not projecting our fears and making assumptions about others. The habit of comparison is difficult to break. There will always be someone more beautiful, happier, more accomplished, and more intelligent. There will always be someone who is less so. The most beautiful moment in life is when we stop and observe whether we are fulfilling our own potential to the best of our ability.

Breaking free means that you are finding your own unique truth. It's easy to adopt external goals based on outside expectations. It's more difficult to create your own set of values. This involves setting goals and defining what's important to you. You follow your own vision by moving forward with your own personally selected goals and not letting any external circumstances circumvent who you are. The process of self-discovery begins with being honest with yourself. This means paying attention. Life is very good at guiding if only we would stop and pay more attention. We can pay attention to a calling we feel. Those are the things you feel are deeply guiding you even if they don't make sense to anyone but yourself. This is about trusting your intuition and knowing when it is time to move on. Your mind may be fighting you, but your soul knows best. The path to inner purpose isn't necessarily linear. Stepping out of your own way is often what allows this type of inner knowing to come through.

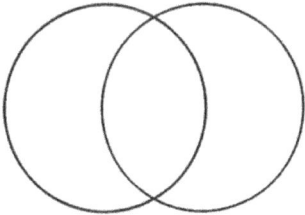

The symbol you see represents two circles becoming creation (or one) through the *vesica piscis*. The interpenetration of the two circles representing two wholes becomes a birth portal. The vesica piscis is about taking action by cocreating an expression of your truth. The potential that emerges from this portal transforms into growth and greater understanding. This is the birthing place of people and ideals, of coming together in mutual understanding and on common ground. As we self-actualize, we become in touch with the internal reference point of the soul rather than the ego. Our intent is the mechanism by which the immaterial transforms into the material. There's the saying "Energy flows to where attention goes." Whatever you pay attention to becomes energized. Attention activates the energy and information fields. When you speak, you transmit information through energy using sound waves. When you send an e-mail, you transmit energy and information. The words you select when you speak and write carry intention.

We've heard a lot about the power of intention and how we can tap into the law of attraction to get what we want. Lynne McTaggart wrote a popular book, *The Intention Experiment*, in which she took the findings from around the world of some of the world's leading scientists on the subject of human consciousness, and she showed us how thought generates its own palpable energy that can be used to improve life and change the world. In religions across the globe, the act of prayer is a common thread that ties humanity together. The power of prayer comes from setting a deep intention and putting energy around it. Intention is very real, and the more we learn to tap into our ability to make strong intentions that are in alignment with our higher selves, the more inner and outer success we will begin to manifest in our lives. All activity in the universe is generated by intention. Intent orchestrates creativity in the universe. The universe responds to our intent when we have an intimate relationship with the universe, and instead of seeing it as separate, we see it as an extension of our body.

Changing the Brain

All acts of creation are an art form and involve the expression of who you are into a more physical manifestation. Self-awareness means that we have a healthy idea of who we are. We are aware of the things that cause us to react and limit us from reaching our potential. We are not prisoners of our limitations. The concept of neuroplasticity—the brain's ability to restructure itself—has completely revolutionized the way we view self-development today. Otherwise known as brain plasticity, it refers to the changes that occur in neural pathways and synapses due to changes in behavior, environment, neural processing, and sometimes injury. If we once believed that the brain was a static organ that physiologically didn't change, we now know that it is constantly evolving throughout our lives. This is a huge paradigm shift. For most of the twentieth century, neuroscientists believed that the brain was largely immutable after a critical stage in early childhood. This old paradigm has been taken over by research that shows that many parts of the brain remain plastic, even into adulthood. Individual connections within the brain are constantly being removed or recreated depending on how we're using them. Deepak Chopra, coauthor of *Superbrain*, outlined this concept in the following way:[clxvi]

1 Your brain can heal its wounds from the past.
2 Your brain is constantly renewing itself.
3 Experience changes the brain every day.
4 The input you give your brain causes it to form new neural pathways.
5 The more positive the input, the better your brain will function.

The more we practice certain responses, the more ingrained and grooved they become in the neural pathways of our brain. Although it's a fairly new paradigm in the field of psychology, you can see that it's intuitively been around for a long time. Take, for instance, Tibetan Buddhism. Various studies have been performed on the brain during meditation (which is a vital part of the Tibetan Buddhist practice). Studies show that the brain does indeed change with a little bit of training and work. Changing your brain does involve a certain level of deeply looking at your personal belief systems. What are the roots of your conditioning? Do they come from a religion, your education, family, media, or your genetics? By looking deeply at yourself, you become empowered through your growing self-awareness.

Our thoughts throughout the day have become habits. Each thought produces a biochemical reaction in the brain, and by having the same thoughts day in and out, our brains have the same reactions. The brain then sends chemical signals in the body. Those thoughts become things. Every thought we carry shapes our brain; what we repeatedly think is where we repeatedly shine our light, and, neurologically, that's who we become. With enough repetition, this becomes tattooed into the fabric of our brain and becomes our habits, patterns, and tendencies. If we are unconsciously creating who we are (and who we no longer perhaps want to be), then we can also literally reinvent ourselves.

In the Hindu scriptures, the concept of neuroplasticity can be looked at from the viewpoint of yoga's central teaching. *Guna* refers to a strand, and in the *Bhagavad Gita*, the gunas are described as the fabric of existence. This is the veil that hides unity in a covering of diversity. Gunas can be seen in different levels of consciousness. *Tamas*, the lowest level, represents the vast unconscious. It is similar to Jung's "collective unconscious" in that it holds the information of our evolutionary heritage. This is a record shared by all humans and is, at its deepest level, universal. In Tamas, there is ignorance of the unity in life. *Rajas* are the mind, or the constant, racing streams of thought. Rajas are uncontrolled and egocentric. *Sattva*, the higher mind, is detached and self-controlled. This is the natural characteristic that comes from unity or purpose. The Gunas describe the basic forces of personality and allow the possibility of shaping ourselves after a higher ideal. Personality is a process, and the human being is constantly in a process of remaking him or herself. If it is left to itself, the mind repeats the same patterns of personality. The central principle of yoga teaches that by training the mind, anyone can change his or her old ways of thinking: "Reshape yourself through the power of your will; never let yourself be degraded by self-will. The will is the only friend of the Self, and the will is the only enemy of the Self."[clxvii]

The Gita speaks of this process as a part of spiritual evolution. Evolution is the slow return to our native state. The Tamas must first be transformed into Rajas, which must then be harnessed to a higher ideal by the will. This becomes Sattva, which channels into selfless action. This is the state of a calm mind and abundant vitality.

The end, though, is a return to unity to still the mind. This is the state of permanent joy.

Dr. Joe Dispenza, author of *Breaking the Habit of Being Yourself*, describes how we become addicted to the emotional conditions and chemicals that create our state of being. We become addicted to ourselves, our routines, and our ways of thinking, feeling, and behaving. We know that any chemical that alters our state of mind (good or bad) can become addictive. Our bodies follow our brains, and our bodies go on to create cell receptor sites that mirror our habits and thoughts to the point that we become these habits and thoughts.[clxviii] If we have, on average, 70,000 thoughts one day, there's a good chance that up to 98% of them are exactly the same thoughts we had the previous day. However, we can change, and, according to Dr. Dispenza, this means that we have to be greater than our environment. For the Hindu sages, this meant silencing the mind through the process of deep meditation. We can bring this into our everyday modern lifestyle. Becoming greater than our environment is possible if we follow three simple rules:

1. **Mindfulness:** Whatever we turn our attention to is what we bring to life. If I told you to focus on your nose, you'd probably quickly become aware that your nose didn't really "exist" until I told you to turn your attention to it. Mindfulness means paying attention to everything you're paying attention to. You can choose, in each moment, to create a new experience in your mind. By bringing something new to your life, you're literally rewiring the thinking process in your brain.

2. **Finding your purpose:** Purpose fuels change. Wanting to feel better or happier isn't enough. This is why living your purpose is of such fundamental importance.

3. **Focusing on your purpose:** When we become focused on our purpose, our brain does not distinguish what is actually real and what is only real in the mind. Our thoughts, therefore, become our experience. To know that neurological change can occur even in the absence of physical interaction is absolutely critical in

understanding how we can change our lives. If you can influence your brain to change before you experience your desired future outcome, then the appropriate neural circuits will be created in your brain and will enable you to become so in alignment with your intention that this new hardware is installed in preparation for the actual manifestation of the event in the future.

By continuously working to refine your neural network, you can create a whole new software in your brain that behaves in a completely new way. The more you clarify and formulate the vision you have in your mind, the easier it will become to manifest this vision into reality. Your brain can be a map to your future. By clarifying your vision or intention, by refining it to align with the highest vision of yourself, and then visualizing and believing it, you will begin to change your mind to reflect the manifestation of your vision into reality and actualize it in its material form.

If you were to imagine how it would feel to be like the person you most greatly admire, this contemplation alone is already firing up new pathways and ways of being in your mind. If you reflect on what it would feel like for you to be totally happy and fulfilled in your life, what is that creation in your mind of that new you? The meditative process can help bring in all the information learned about what it means for you to be totally fulfilled and living your purpose. You can be selective of the type of experience you want to create for yourself and begin to activate the circuitry of your mind. It is also important for you to remind yourself to not be enslaved to your emotions of the past. Instead, focus on elevated emotions (such as love and gratitude) and experience those emotions in relation to the creation of the vision you have in your future. Meditation will help you move from the state of thinking to that of being.

The Identity Gap

Dr. Dispenza talks about an "identity gap" that many of us experience. This is the gap between how we appear to others in our environment (i.e., who we project to the outside) and who we really are (how we feel on the inside). The narrower our gaps, the closer we are to our own truth and authenticity. When we pick up emotional states, such as guilt, shame, anger, fear, depression, and judgment, we begin to develop a gap between who we are and the way we appear to others.[clxix] We wear various emotions in layers and become attached to them. They become our "identity."

When we are young, we experience events that later define us and contribute to our emotional makeup. We stay busy "doing" things and begin to sweep our old emotions under the rug. We experience a myriad of events that produce a myriad of emotions, and eventually they begin to define who we are. By our mid-30s to 40s, our personalities are almost fully complete. We've probably settled into a career and had several relationships. By this time, we know what both loss and success feel like, as well as what we like or dislike. We begin to predict the emotions we will feel in advance of an event even occurring. Because of this, we also know how to make the feelings about who we are go away. By midlife, we're most likely living in the environment we've created during our lives to erase any feelings of pain or guilt that we carry.

To effectively rewire the neural circuitry in your brain, it is important to look at the negative emotional states that have had an impact on your life and become so familiar with them that you can observe whenever they occur. By observing these states, you will use them to unmemorize the negative emotional states and surrender to a greater mind. This will begin to close the gap between who you really are and who you have presented to the world. By closing the gap, we release the energy that was once used to produce the feelings. With freed-up energy, you can use it in creativity and life purpose. You can allow yourself to break free. Open yourself up to the universal intelligence that we can all access, and free yourself from the jailed confines of conditioning and limitation.

CHAPTER 7

Meditation: Healing Medicine for Humanity

From the Hindu tantric tradition comes the symbol of the *Sri Yantra*. Its nine interlocking triangles form a powerful symbol for meditation. The nine triangles are interlaced in such a way as to form 43 smaller triangles in a web that is symbolic of the entire cosmos or a womb that is symbolic of creation. Together, they express *non-duality*. These triangles are surrounded by a lotus of eight petals, a lotus of sixteen petals, and an earth square resembling a temple with four doors. The proportions of the largest triangle are the same as each face of the Great Pyramid of Giza in Egypt. The dimensions of that pyramid also conform to the proportion of the Phi ratio.[clxx]

Some of the earliest written records of meditation come from the *Hindu* traditions of *Vedantism* from around 1500 BCE.[clxxi] The *Vedas* discuss the meditative traditions of *ancient India*. Around the 6th to

5th centuries BCE, other forms of meditation developed in *Taoist* China and *Buddhist* India. Meditation is a powerful tool. It allows us to place our attention and intention on the more subtle planes, and this is where we gain access to untapped energy. On the Sri Yantra, this is symbolized by the nine interlocking triangles that surround and radiate out from the central point, which is the junction between the physical universe and its unmanifest source.

The sages of the Upanishads looked inward to analyze the data that nature presents to the mind. They found not a world of separate objects but a ceaseless process of change—matter coming together and dissolving into a different form. They found a changeless, infinite, indivisible reality, which they called *Brahman* of the divine ground of existence. In contemporary physics, we are reminded that the things we see "out there" are not ultimately separate from each other and from us. We perceive them as such because of the limitations of our senses. If our eyes were more sensitive to a finer spectrum, we would see the world as a continuous field of energy and matter. Through the course of history, this tenet can be found worldwide among anyone who has experienced these depths of consciousness. Ruysbroek, a great mystic of medieval Europe, wrote, "The Image of God is found essentially and personally in all mankind. Each possesses it whole, entire and undivided, and all together not more than one alone. In this way we are all one, intimately united in our eternal image, which is the image of God and the source in us of all our life.[clxxii]"

What the sages found by testing each level of awareness is that in a supreme climax of meditation (when consciousness is so focused that it is completely withdrawn from body and mind), one enters a state of singularity in which the ego disappears. They discovered a core of consciousness beyond time and change and called this *Atman* or Self. The sages discovered that in profound meditation, there was *unity* known as *advaita* or "not two." The *Chandogya Upanishad* says *Tat tvam asi*, which means "Thou art that." Atman and Brahman are one. The Self in each person is not different from the Godhead.

Non-dual awareness is available to us at all times, and yet, the human propensity is to go back and construct our experiences in terms of a singular and separate self. The goal of meditation in all enlightenment traditions is to extinguish this latent potential. With that, we extinguish suffering. One of the approaches of meditation is to change the very experience of self, not just as an altered state of consciousness. This is to shift the center point of subjective thought from representation of self to awareness of self. One asks, "Who is it that is thinking this, feeling this, experiencing this, behaving in this way?" This leads to detaching our Self from awareness and coming to a realization that we are awareness itself. Another approach is to direct our awareness to the moment-to-moment manifestation and experience of the self. This is the basis of all forms of Buddhist mindfulness practice: *Vipassana* in Theravada Buddhism and *Mahamudra* in Vajrayana Buddhism.

Different forms of mindfulness meditation arose from the various teachings of Buddha. In general, the practitioner practices attending to deeper aspects of perception, starting with breathing and ending with the awareness of an impermanence of all things and the lack of separation between one's self, others, and the world. Mindfulness can be experienced while walking, eating, or running errands.[clxxiii] What's similar in the yogic-meditative practices of Tibetan Mahamudra practice, Hindu Raj Yoga, and Theravada vipassana meditation is that it is meditation that allows one to experience the conceptual-perceptual process. In this process we dualistically structure our experiences in terms of self and objects. We project a "thingness" onto things, thereby bringing the self (in the inner world) and the material realm (the outer world) into a moment-by-moment existence. The division of experience into "self" and "other" comes from the perceptual process itself, in which we become conscious of our perceptions and weave meaning into them. Meditation allows us to get inside the first half of this process, and it gives us a view into what our eyes alone cannot see. We are able to view what the universe looked like in its earlier stages of evolution.

Practice and training are required to get back to the way things are naturally because we tend to make things difficult for ourselves. We have projections, misattributions, dysfunctional beliefs, unsatisfying attachments, wishful thinking, and reenactments of pain. We fight to hold onto what we can, and we resist the challenges against what we perceive as safe and secure. The three major systems of meditation (Hindu Raj Yoga, Tibetan Mahamudra, and Theravada Vipassana) have similar approaches to the step-by-step perceptual process; yet each experiences the nature of change differently. Moment-to-moment vicissitudes in Raj Yoga are experienced as a continuous transformation of *ekatattva*, or the "same stuff." In the selfless Buddhist practice, change is experienced as a succession of *ksanika*, or momentary and discontinuously discrete events. Is reality then continuous or discontinuous?

Quantum physics teaches us that the way in which we set up an experiment affects its outcome. Depending on how we set up our experiment, light can reveal itself to us as wavelike (continuous) or particle-like (discontinuous). The different systems of meditation may reveal to us how we construct our perceptual bias; yet, they all take us back through the process of self and world construction. The point of meditation is to loosen the grip we have on the "I" in order to initiate the opening that allows life to flow unimpeded by the fixations of who "I am."

For us here in the modern world, meditation is the key to quieting our active minds. We are constantly jumping from thought to thought and feeling to feeling, and most of these thoughts and feelings are taking us away from what we want to achieve. Meditation is connecting with that nonlocal intelligence. We need it to move past the distracting thoughts that become a barrier to our truth. When we are quiet, when we experience gaps of silence, we catch glimpses of the deeper levels of our soul. As we catch these glimpses, our consciousness also expands. The purpose of meditation is to stop thinking to allow this barrier to slowly dissolve.

The work of meditation is to make you aware of all the mental chatter that goes on in your mind. When we are able to sit back and observe this chatter, we begin to disidentify. There is nothing more enlightening than the disidentification of freedom and of being a master of one's destiny. When we drop our minds, we open ourselves to the buried wounds of our past, allowing them to rise to the surface to be healed. With openness comes the acceptance to be healed, which then helps others. Becoming aware of our wounds means that we move to our roots. The less we think, the more opportunity there is for healing. Coming from this place, we stop reacting, and an energy flows through us. Osho calls this "living a headless life."[clxxiv]

Meditation brings you into a space of meeting the very soul of silence. In silence, there is nothing to do and nowhere to go. Silence makes many of us very uncomfortable because we are so used to the noise and activity of the world. Silence is where you come home to yourself. The understanding that comes during these moments is what manifests in the physical realm. Silence is the same for all. Rather than constantly striving for a life of activity, one must recognize that the deepest wisdom arises in moments of silence.

Today, meditation is becoming a fashion statement. With evidence mounting that meditation can enhance our memory, creativity, compassion, productivity, and even intelligence, some of the most groundbreaking companies out there are incorporating mindfulness into their corporate programs. Google incorporates a mindfulness course into the company called "Search Inside Yourself" by way of its software engineer Chade-Meng Tan.

Dr. John Lieff describes the effects of meditation on the brain in the following ways:[clxxv]

- **Compassion meditation** increases gamma oscillations, synchrony, and activity in the brain regions that govern empathy. It also increases the thalamus filtering of sensory–motor signals.
- **Mindfulness meditation** increases the number of neurons, axon density, amount of myelin, and the number of connections in the regions of the brain associated with concentration and emotion. It decreases activity in the amygdala regions of stress and increases hippocampal activity in the regions of memory.
- **Transcendental meditation (TM)** increases synchronous oscillations throughout the brain. It has also been shown to have positive heart effects on people who have high blood pressure.
- **Tai chi** increases growth factors that stimulate new brain cells, brain volume, and memory improvement.

- **All meditation** shows changes in the default mode network (DMN), which is the brain circuit that is thought to most closely relate to the sense of who we are. This includes non-focused internal thought, daydreaming, wondering, remembering, future planning, and thinking about others. In all meditation, the DMN is altered (briefly in beginning meditators and permanently in experienced meditators). There is an increase in self-monitoring of thought and emotion, as well as increased control of behavior and thought. Meditation increases the gyrification or folding of the cortex, and the longer one practices, the more gyrification occurs.

Looking at the process of meditation from a scientific standpoint involves looking at the brain. Your brain is made up of billions of brain cells called neurons, which use electricity to communicate with each other. The combination of millions of neurons sending signals at once produces an enormous amount of electrical activity in the brain, which can be detected using sensitive medical equipment (such as an EEG) to measure electricity levels over areas of the scalp. The combination of electrical activity of the brain is commonly called a brain wave pattern because of its cyclic, wave-like nature. The different brain wave frequencies include:[clxxvi]

- **Beta:** This is the state of being wide awake. The mind makes connections quickly and easily, and it is primed to do work that requires full attention. Neurons fire abundantly and in rapid succession, helping you achieve peak performance. Beta waves range from 13–40 Hz. It's associated with peak concentration, heightened alertness, hand-eye coordination, and visual acuity.
- **Alpha:** When you are relaxed, your brain activity slows from the rapid patterns of Beta into the more gentle waves of Alpha. Awareness expands and creative energy begins to flow. Alpha waves range from 7–12 Hz. This is a place of deep relaxation. It is the gateway that leads into deeper states of consciousness. Alpha is also the home of the window frequency known as the Schuman Resonance, which is the resonant frequency of the earth's electromagnetic field.

MEDITATION: HEALING MEDICINE FOR HUMANITY

- **Theta:** Theta takes you even deeper into relaxation, where brain activity slows almost to the point of sleep. Theta brings forward heightened receptivity, flashes of dreamlike imagery, inspiration, and long-forgotten memories. You may feel your mind expand beyond the boundaries of your body. Theta rests directly on the threshold of subconscious. In biofeedback, it is most commonly associated with the deepest levels of meditation. Theta waves range from 4–7 Hz. Theta is known as the twilight state that we normally only experience fleetingly as we rise out of the depths of Delta upon waking or drifting off to sleep. In Theta, we are receptive to information beyond our normal conscious awareness.
- **Delta:** Delta is the slowest of all four brain-wave frequencies. Most commonly associated with deep sleep, certain frequencies in the Delta range also trigger the release of human growth hormone (which is beneficial for healing and regeneration). This is why deep, restorative sleep is essential to the healing process. Delta is the brain-wave signal of the subconscious, from which intuition arises. Delta-based programs are not only an ideal choice for their sleep and deep regeneration potential, but also to access unconscious activity for clearing and empowerment. Delta waves range from 0–4 Hz.

Meditation is not as difficult as some may perceive it to be. It simply takes finding a place where you can sit uninterrupted in a comfortable position. It is recommended that one sit up with eyes closed during the process. When the eyes are closed, the brain begins to block the sensory and environmental input that is coming in through your eyes. Brain waves begin to lessen in frequency, and you begin to move toward the desirable "Alpha state." When you close your eyes, you begin to relax, become less preoccupied with your external world, and begin focusing on your internal world.

As you're sitting with your eyes closed, you begin to witness your breath. You observe the inflow and outflow of the breath and any attempts to control it. Without resistance or judgment, you also observe your thoughts if you have any. When your thoughts begin to take over, you remember to always return to your breath. Awareness of your breathing is the most basic form of meditation. You move from a state of thinking to one of feeling. With meditation, comes awareness, where you become better able to stop yourself from behaving unconsciously. We remember that deep inside we are just witnesses—silent and unchanged. A bridge is unveiled, connecting one from that active state of *thinking and doing* to a non-active state of witnessing. Our minds tend to burden us with memories of the past and projections of the future. When we begin to drop our minds, we gain a new state of awareness that also helps us detach from our desires and expectations.

From an elevated state of mind that comes from a place of gratitude and empowerment. Gandhi once said, "If we could change ourselves, the tendencies in the world would also change. As a man changes his own nature, so does the attitude of the world change toward him." The goal of meditation is simple. Heightening control of the mind allows us to see the world in a much more compassionate way. It helps us break down the categorizations we have that often divide people from each other. Remind yourself that all things in the material world come from an invisible field in the immaterial, and by planting the seeds you wish to plant in the world, you are also seeing them bear fruit. If you can learn to experience a vision so intensely in your inner field of potential, then know that it has already happened. We are divine creators. Because we are creatures of habit, make your habits ones of compassion, creativity, love, gratitude, and empowerment. Begin to believe that you can do and be anything. You don't have to cater to the impositions of society. It's time to take charge and begin the process that will change the rest of your life.

CHAPTER 8

Storytelling for Future Generations

The book ends with the *merkaba*, which is the star tetrahedron. The upward-facing tetrahedron represents male, fire, and a blade, while the downward-pointing tetrahedron represents female, water, and the chalice. They interlock together creating the interpenetration of male and female, and a dynamic balance of expanded awareness. This is one of the primary geometries of the human energy field, which, when activated, forms a time–space vehicle toward ascension. The merkaba is the mer(light)-ka(spirit)-ba(body) in a sacred union. This is where we connect to the higher part of our being and tap into universal wisdom. This is about shifting individual and planetary consciousness from duality to unity. This is the unity that honors our journey of expansion. We are stepping into the outer limits of human potential.

The stories we find in the vibrant oral cultural traditions serve as a medicine for humanity and the world. Different symbols and archetypes hold great power for the individual at certain times in his or her journey. Archetypes provide directions for growth and play a role in our self-awareness. The stories in this book are intended to empower healing individually and of the world. In merging the old and the new, one may gain greater access to the wisdom within—the wisdom of our earth.

According to an old Scottish proverb, a story is "told eye to eye, mind to mind, and heart to heart." Storytelling creates a bridge between the teller and the listener across which authentic communication can take place. Storyteller Diane Rooks said, "Stories can change the way we see our lives and the world. Using metaphor and imagery, stories offer healing and growth to everyone, those who tell them and those who listen. They connect us to each other and help us find meaning as we imagine new possibilities and find hope.[clxxvii]"

A few years ago, The Annals of Internal Medicine published a study examining the effects of storytelling on patients with *high blood pressure*[clxxviii]. Stories are an essential part of how we communicate, interpret experiences, and incorporate new information into our lives. Experts in this emerging field of narrative communication say that storytelling effectively counteracts the initial denial that can arise when a patient learns of a new diagnosis or is asked to change deeply ingrained behaviors. "Telling and listening to stories is the way we make sense of our lives," said Dr. Thomas K. Houston, lead author of the study and a researcher at the University of Massachusetts Medical School in Worcester and the Veterans Affairs medical center in Bedford, Mass. "That natural tendency may have the potential to alter behavior and improve health[clxxix]."

Storytelling has often played an essential role in indigenous cultures. Stories for healing contain many of the values that are an important part of many native cultures like acceptance, courage, truth, and spirituality. Through stories, people are often able to make sense of their own experiences. We are beginning to recognize, more and more, the healing power of the narrative as tools in modern behavioral health practice. As they become understood, these indigenous healing methods are gaining respect as powerful tools for healing.

STORYTELLING FOR FUTURE GENERATIONS

Traditionally, indigenous cultures understood the importance of spiritual balance for individual and community well-being. There was an understanding that ceremonies were part of the ongoing fabric of the community and existed to prepare, protect, and heal the individual as he or she journeyed through life's stages. Ceremonies often marked specific rites of passage, where a person would be preparing to give up 'old' roles and responsibilities and embrace a set of new ones.

Social entrepreneur Brenda Laurel said, "Stories are tools for knowing and judging. Change the stories and you change how people live[clxxx]." Decades ago, it would have been hard to imagine that apartheid in South Africa would fall. There was a relatively peaceful transition out of apartheid into democracy partly from a unique project in 1992 that brought together a group of diverse South Africans to imagine the country's future. They included businesses, citizens, leaders from both left and right, and enemies. Together, they created something called the Mont Fleur Scenarios in which they imaged South Africa's evolution over the coming decades.

The Ostrich, they imagined, was a future in which the white government stuck their heads in the sand. Inaction would eventually lead to civil war. Lame Duck was a weak government that prolonged the transition by trying to do too much, thus accomplishing very little. Icarus was a future in which a black government came to power, but eventually crashed (along with the economy). Flight of the Flamingos was a future based on positive transition. It was symbolic of the flock of flamingos eventually flying off together[clxxxi]. When the Mont Fleur Scenarios were released, people suddenly had four paths to think about and debate. Because the stories were simple and easily relatable, they spread quickly. They shaped policy options and negotiations. People actually came together. Since this project, imagining shared futures have become an important tool for bringing about social change in the world.

If we hope to live in the true consciousness of our existence, one of our greatest achievements is to find meaning in life. Wisdom is built from small step to small step, from the irrational beginnings of childhood. Many parents project their wishes and expectations onto children, to be and act a certain way. One of the most important tasks in parenting is to help your child find meaning in life. In order to achieve this, certain growth experiences are necessary. The child slowly learns to understand him or herself better and thus to better understand others. Eventually, the child is able to relate to others in mutually meaningful ways.

To find meaning, one must often leap from the narrow confines of self-centered existence to a belief that one will contribute something great to life. We must learn to develop our inner resources so that creativity and intellect can mutually support each other. Of the experiences that help bring children the sense of meaning, the stories told through oral tradition or literature carry this information in some of the most effective ways. What are the stories we tell our children to help them develop the inner resources they will need as they go through life?

Children have often found meaning through fairy tales. These are the stories that capture their attention and arouse their curiosity. The German poet Schiller once wrote, "Deeper meaning resides in the fairy tales told to me in my childhood than in the truth that is taught by life."[clxxxii] Storytelling carries important messages to the conscious, the preconscious, and the unconscious. These stories help children become aware of the universal problems and speak to their budding ego and development. They may speak to the inner pressures that children feel in a way that their subconscious understands.

When I look at the world through the eyes of my three-year-old son, I see his intimacy with everything around him. He sees the tiny stones and flowers, and he hears the birds that I no longer notice. In childhood, we see the power of the dream, fairy tales, and myths— the parallel worlds that exist at once. We constantly drift from one world to the other. At some point in adulthood, our awareness changes. We learn to separate ourselves from each other and the world around us.

In one of my earlier stories, I described the process of the "Awakening the Dreamer: Changing the Dreamer" symposium. For adults, these stories help us examine our assumptions and wake up from the trance of the modern world. We can similarly share the stories with our children to help them understand their place in and contribution to the world. Often, as parents, we don't want our children to know that the source of what goes wrong in life is due to our own nature: our aggression, our materialism, our excesses, and our selfishness. Children need to continue to be nurtured with the stories of heroes who go out into the world, and although they are initially ignorant about many things, they must find their path by following their hearts with inner confidence.

Storyteller and author Virginia Driving Hawk Sneve talks about how, as an eager young girl, she would listen to her grandmother tell the story of Lakota culture. In an article about native storytellers connecting past and future, Shannon Smith writes, "The silence between the words of the story envelops the children, stirring their souls as they sit around their elder. Their fathers are away from the village hunting for dinner, their mothers are preparing the tepees, their grandmothers are writing history into the air and into minds as their words call out to the children. Words of meaning, words of instruction, stories showing where people come from, how they are, what they should be.[clxxxiii]"

Storytelling is writing the past, living the present, and preserving the future. Storytelling is a way to further the continuation of life in modern society.

Today, in modern society, children no longer grow up within the security of an extended family or a well-integrated community. It is more important than ever to provide the modern child with images of heroes and heroines who, following the call, have gone out into the world. We, as adults, must go through our own journey by recovering the sacred, taking the ancient wisdom found in some of the "old-growth cultures," and passing this wisdom onto our children. This is a critical point in history and is what humanity needs most.

We must retrieve the teachings that tell us that what we do to the earth, we do to ourselves. We must also live with our eyes on the horizon of seven generations to come. In sharing the stories that celebrate our interdependence and interconnection with the diversity of life, we sow the seeds with the intention that the fertile soil on which they land will enable them to sprout and spread. For Six Nations people, the law of the seed honors the natural cycles of creation and regeneration. Seeds carry life from generation to generation with no end. Every time we plant a seed, they become a life, which then become our ancestors for generations to come.

Progress involves multiple steps. The first is to develop our own awareness. Our decisions affect everything around us, and we can become stewards of the earth if we so wish. The next step is coming together as a social movement. People are starting to wake up and recognize the need for change. For life to continue as we wish, we need to change our dream from that of materialism and domination to one of cooperation and earth-honoring. When people from vastly different backgrounds come together, the result is a sharing of wisdom and commitment. In combining what we have learned in the modern world, through our educational systems, with the stories of creation and our subconscious, we can move toward a sustainable and healthy future.

In ending, let us look to these stories, symbols, wisdom teachings and embody them in everything we do. The sacred path of eco-consciousness translates into one thing: the psychological health of our modern world is directly tied to the health of the earth. Those who see themselves in all and all in them would not be capable of harming others. Human destiny rests in human hands. We shape ourselves and our world by what we believe, think, and act on. This understanding is essential to our healing. What did *you* do, once you knew?

In *Lak'ech Ala K'in*–I am another you.

CHAPTER 9

The Journey Continues

My intention for this book is to inspire you to commit to a new story for humanity that values connection and cooperation. It is to encourage you to utilize your unique gifts to transform the systems and structures that oppress and separate us. Transforming the world is a team sport. Discover what you feel called to do, in a way that only you can do it. Ask yourself, "What will I do?" In ending, I would like to offer you a plan of action that offers ideas and strategies for ensuring the healing of ourselves, and the planet.

The Outer World

1. Be mindful of how we let our things define us. Think about what you buy, use, keep, throw away, waste, and save. The material things that flow through our lives are an indication of the type of lives we lead. There is a secret life behind everything you own, and most of the time, it's not pretty.
2. Ask yourself how much you really need. The relationship between material wealth and wellbeing is only proportional to a certain point, and then the pattern becomes inversely proportional.
3. Be mindful of your consumption. According to happiness researchers, we are less happy than we used to be. One of the leading causes of unhappiness in developed nations is our overabundance of choice. Too many options actually bring about increased rates of stress, anxiety, and uncertainty[clxxxiv]. Keep a healthy distance between yourself, and the seductions of advertising that bombard us.
4. Buy socially and environmentally responsible apparel (sweatshop-free labor, renewable fibers, organic cotton, hemp, modal, lyocell, bamboo fiber, and merino wool clothing options).
5. Use nontoxic products to clean your home. Not only is it healthier for you, but also better for the environment.
6. Support local farmers, promote organic agriculture, and decrease your reliance on franchised eateries for sustenance. Buy foods that promote sustainable farming. Buy fair-trade coffee, chocolate, and bananas.
7. Teach children to develop a more intimate connection with the source of their food. The more they understand where their food is coming from, the more mindful they become about what they eat.
8. Think about how you can support the sustainable future of food. Buy meat and seafood from sustainable ranchers and fisheries.
9. Keep a seed bank to preserve humanity's agricultural heritage.
10. Drive a hybrid or biodiesel car.

11 Green your home, conserve electricity, and water. Don't use more than you need.

12 Build community: empower the younger generation, support each other, promote education, improve health care, and take on holistic approaches to solve challenges.

13 Encourage social entrepreneurship. If even a small percentage of our entrepreneurial capacities were directed toward creating social value above economic value, this world would be a very different place.

14 Make socially responsible investments to change the world.

15 Ask yourself if an industry or company is contributing to reducing the world's problems and support those that do.

16 Learn about the inner workings of our systems, governments, and corporations.

17 Examine your assumptions. Attend an Awakening the Dreamer: Changing the Dream Symposium (*http://www.uptous.org/symposium*).

18 Find an opportunity to improve something and jump on it. New business ideas can be profitable and change the world.

19 Optimism can be revolutionary, and the greatest movements for social change began with an optimistic view that better solutions are available, action is possible, and people can come together and act our their highest principles. Build a movement of change, not apathy.

20 Come together with others and build a vision of the future together, letting go of the past.

21 Use the Internet to influence political and economic structures. Use it as a platform to engage in conversations about the challenges of our society. Form friendships and alliances across borders. Engage in social technology to let your voice be heard.

22 Change occurs when we speak up. Write letters to your politicians. Use the tools available to talk about the things that need improving.

23 Take political action through music, films, art, and writing.

24. Think about what you do for a living. The professions that help people cope with change are going to see an increased demand.
25. Go to *SafeClimate.net*'s carbon-footprint calculator and figure out your environmental footprint.

The Inner World

1. Meditation is not about following a specific religion or spiritual practice. It doesn't necessarily have to be done while sitting cross-legged on the floor either. You can meditate while you're cleaning, or taking a walk. Meditation is about incorporating a mindfulness practice into your life that involves calming your thoughts and emotions, allowing you to be in the present moment. If you're interested in starting a meditation practice, there are many resources out there to help you on your path.
2. Practice gratitude. Think about all the things in your life you appreciate regularly.
3. Instead of reading the mainstream news, find uplifting stories that you can read and share with others.
4. Cut back on the amount of television you watch, and decrease the amount of time you spend plugged into social networking sites. Reduce mindless consumption of media and news.
5. Sit and watch nature. Get yourself in touch with your natural surroundings. Listen to the birds. Spend at least five minutes a day in this practice.
6. Exercise doesn't mean getting sweaty at the gym. It can be about taking a gentle walk outside, and becoming calm and alert. Spend some time every day to move your body through some form of exercise.
7. Listen to uplifting and inspiring music, it's a great way to get yourself back in the present moment.
8. Practice random acts of kindness.

9. Become aware of your thoughts. If they're negative, make a conscious effort to turn it into a loving voice.
10. If you're stressed out, find practices that relax you. It may be something like lighting a candle, taking a bath, or listening to relaxing music.
11. Create something that will inspire others.
12. Take deep breaths. Connect yourself to the ground regularly and just breathe.
13. Be true to yourself, and find ways to keep your inner ideals in line with the way you behave.
14. Have a sense of humor about life, and laugh a lot. It's a great stress antidote and helps us relax.
15. Live in the moment. Instead of worrying about the past or future, really enjoy the now.
16. Worry less. We have between 30,000 – 75,000 thoughts per day, of which 80% are random nonsensical thoughts. Learn to recognize unnecessary worries.
17. There are some things that you just cannot change, no matter how hard you try. Learn to detach and let things go.
18. Guilt is a toxic emotion. Stop putting unnecessary pressure on yourself.
19. Connect with others of like mind.
20. Find positive outlets for your negative emotions, so that you are not suppressing things.
21. Stop and slow down. It's okay to be still and quiet.
22. Stop comparing yourself to others, the most important thing is that you are being true to yourself and living the life you want.
23. Remember that less is more, and the simple things in life are what bring us the most happiness.
24. Make it a habit to examine your judgments, assumptions, and perspectives. Often, we are projecting our own fears onto other people and circumstances.

25 Spend quality time with your children. Become mindful of when you are using technology to keep them (or yourself) occupied.

26 Material things cause us stress because we cling to them, in fear of losing them. Understand the consumerism trap, and simplify your life.

27 Practice self-care. Create rituals for nourishing your mind and body.

28 Get in touch with your inner purpose and passions.

29 Understand that in order to see the change you want in the world, you have to first embody that change yourself.

30 The seeds we choose to sow today, will affect us seven generations to come.

Bibliography

i   Elgin, Duane (2009). The Living Universe: Where Are We? Who Are We? Where Are We Going?; Berrett-Koehler Publishers, p. 2

ii   Tolle, Eckart (2004). The Power of Now: A Guide to Spiritual Enlightenment; New World Library

iii   Nelson, Melissa K (2008). Original Instructions: Indigenous Teachings for a Sustainable Future; Bear & Company

iv   International Council for Science / Conseil International pour la Science (March 2002). "Science and Traditional Knowledge: Report from the ICSU Study Group on Science and Traditional Knowledge". p. 3. Retrieved 24 May 2012.

v   http://www.shamanicjourney.com/article/6090/spiritual-traditions-of-the-andes-interview-with-doris-rivera-lenz-part-1

vi   Pinkola Estés, Clarissa (1996). Women who Run with the Wolves: Myths and Stories of the Wild Woman Archetype; Ballantine Books

vii   Perkins, John (April 1, 1994). The World Is As You Dream It: Teachings from the Amazon and Andes; Destiny Books, p. 126

viii   http://www.nationalgeographic.com/adventure/0603/features/peru.html

ix   Narby, Jeremy and Jeremy P. Tarcher (1999).The Cosmic Serpent: DNA and the Origins of Knowledge; Putnam

x   *http://www.takiwasi.com/docs/urti_ing/ayahuasca_helps_cure_drug_addiction.pdf*

xi   http://www.nationalgeographic.com/adventure/0603/features/peru2.html

xii   http://www.nationalgeographic.com/adventure/0603/features/peru2.html

xiii   http://www.maps.org/ayahuasca/Thomas_et_al_CDAR.pdf

xiv   http://www.nationalgeographic.com/adventure/0603/features/peru2.html

xv   http://www.nationalgeographic.com/adventure/0603/features/peru2.html

xvi   Strassman, Rick, M.D. (2000). DMT: The Spirit Molecule: A Doctor's Revolutionary Research into the Biology of Near-Death and Mystical Experiences; Park Street Press

xvii   Strassman, Rick, M.D. (2000). DMT: The Spirit Molecule: A Doctor's Revolutionary Research into the Biology of Near-Death and Mystical Experiences; Park Street Press

xviii   Strassman, Rick, M.D. (2000). DMT: The Spirit Molecule: A Doctor's Revolutionary Research into the Biology of Near-Death and Mystical Experiences; Park Street Press

xix   Elgin, Duane (2009). The Living Universe: Where Are We? Who Are We? Where Are We Going?; Berrett-Koehler Publishers, p. 37

xx   http://www.thepathofthesun.com/2012/09/the-sacred-medicine-ayahuasca.html

xxi   http://www.nbcnews.com/id/23468364/ns/technology_and_science-science/t/was-moses-high-mount-sinai/#.UkC6PhaRh8s

xxii   http://www.livescience.com/38215-cavemen-painted-high.html

xxiii   Narby, Jeremy (1999). The Cosmic Serpent: DNA and the Origins of Knowledge; Penguin

xxiv   Campbell, Joseph (1968). Occidental Mythology: The Masks of God; Penguin, p. 154

xxv   Tzu, Chuang (1998). The Inner Chapters; Counterpoint, p. 43

xxvi   Narby, Jeremy (1999). The Cosmic Serpent: DNA and the Origins of Knowledge; Penguin, p. 86

xxvii   Pollack, Robert (1994). Signs of Life: The Language and Meanings of DNA; Mariner, pp. 29–30

xxviii   Narby, Jeremy (1999). The Cosmic Serpent: DNA and the Origins of Knowledge; Penguin, p. 92

xxix   Eliade, Mircea (1959). The Sacred and the Profane: The Nature of Religion; Houghton Mifflin Harcourt, pp. 52–53

xxx   Narby, Jeremy (1999). The Cosmic Serpent: DNA and the Origins of Knowledge; Penguin, pp. 116–117

xxxi   Hart, Francene. Sacred Geometry (http://www.francenehart.com/sacgeo.htm)

xxxii   New International Version, Luke 6:38

xxxiii   http://www.urbanbaby.com/topics/53801088

xxxiv   *http://www.realitysandwich.com/sacred_economics_ch_21_working_gift_pt_22*

xxxv   http://www.realitysandwich.com/gift_economics_and_reunion_digital_age

xxxvi   English Standard Version, Luke 6:31

xxxvii   http://worldwildlife.org/threats/deforestation

xxxviii   http://en.wikipedia.org/wiki/Achuar_people

BIBLIOGRAPHY

xxxix   http://www.pachamama.org/news/ecuadors-protracted-xi-oil-round-auction-deemed-a-flop

xl   Twist, Lynne (2006). The Soul of Money: Reclaiming the Wealth of Our Inner Resources; W. W. Norton & Company

xli   Twist, Lynne (2006). The Soul of Money: Reclaiming the Wealth of Our Inner Resources; W. W. Norton & Company

xlii   Twist, Lynne (2006). The Soul of Money: Reclaiming the Wealth of Our Inner Resources; W. W. Norton & Company

xliii   Perkins, John (2005). Confessions of an Economic Hit Man; Plume

xliv   Perkins, John (2005). Confessions of an Economic Hit Man; Plume

xlv   Perkins, John (2005). Confessions of an Economic Hit Man; Plume

xlvi   Perkins, John (2005). Confessions of an Economic Hit Man; Plume

xlvii   Perkins, John (2005). Confessions of an Economic Hit Man; Plume

xlviii   Perkins, John (2005). Confessions of an Economic Hit Man; Plume

xlix   Perkins, John (2005). Confessions of an Economic Hit Man; Plume

l   Perkins, John (2005). Confessions of an Economic Hit Man; Plume

li   McLamb, Eric (September 18, 2011). The Ecological Impact of the Industrial Revolution; Ecology Global Network; http://www.ecology.com/2011/09/18/ecological-impact-industrial-revolution/

lii   World Wildlife Fund (WWF), Global Footprint Network (GFN) and ZSL Living Conservation (2010). Living Planet Report

liii   Ewing, Brad (2010). The Ecological Footprint Atlas 2010; Global Footprint Network

liv   World Wildlife Fund (WWF), Global Footprint Network (GFN) and ZSL Living Conservation (2010). Living Planet Report

lv   Organization for Economic Co-operation Development (OECD) (2012). OECD Environmental Outlook to 2050: The Consequences of Inaction; DOI: 10.1787/9789264122246-en

lvi   Organization for Economic Co-operation Development (OECD) (2012). OECD Environmental Outlook to 2050: The Consequences of Inaction; DOI: 10.1787/9789264122246-en

lvii   http://www.oecd.org/general/listofoecdmembercountries-ratificationoftheconventionontheoecd.htm

lviii   Organization for Economic Co-operation Development (OECD) (2012). OECD Environmental Outlook to 2050: The Consequences of Inaction; DOI: 10.1787/9789264122246-en

lix	Organization for Economic Co-operation Development (OECD) (2012). OECD Environmental Outlook to 2050: The Consequences of Inaction; DOI: 10.1787/9789264122246-en
lx	Steffen, Alex (2008). WorldChanging: A User's Guide for the 21st Century; Abrams
lxi	Experts actually call this natural extinction rate the background extinction rate. This simply means the rate of species extinctions that would occur if humans were not around.
lxii	Between 1.4 and 1.8 million species have already been scientifically identified.
lxiii	http://wwf.panda.org/about_our_earth/biodiversity/biodiversity/
lxiv	Abramsky, Sasha (2013). The American Way of Poverty: How the Other Half Still Lives; Nation Books
lxv	http://articles.washingtonpost.com/2013-09-10/opinions/41917153_1_income-inequality-reich-sharknado
lxvi	http://www.nytimes.com/2012/10/17/business/economy/income-inequality-may-take-toll-on-growth.html?pagewanted=all&_r=0
lxvii	http://www.nytimes.com/2012/10/17/business/economy/income-inequality-may-take-toll-on-growth.html?pagewanted=all&_r=0
lxviii	http://stats.oecd.org/Index.aspx?DataSetCode=CWB
lxix	http://www.nytimes.com/2013/07/31/business/economy/in-us-an-inequality-gap-of-sobering-breadth.html
lxx	http://stats.oecd.org/Index.aspx?DataSetCode=CWB
lxxi	http://www.oecd.org/pisa/pisaproducts/48852584.pdf
lxxii	http://milescorak.com/2012/05/02/inequality-and-social-mobility/
lxxiii	http://stats.oecd.org/Index.aspx?DataSetCode=IDD
lxxiv	http://www.oecd-ilibrary.org/social-issues-migration-health/government-social-spending_20743904-table1
lxxv	http://www.slate.com/articles/health_and_science/medical_examiner/2013/04/diagnostic_and_statistical_manual_fifth_edition_why_will_half_the_u_s_population.html
lxxvi	http://www.slate.com/articles/health_and_science/medical_examiner/2013/04/diagnostic_and_statistical_manual_fifth_edition_why_will_half_the_u_s_population.html
lxxvii	http://www.slate.com/articles/health_and_science/medical_examiner/2013/04/diagnostic_and_statistical_manual_fifth_edition_why_will_half_the_u_s_population.html

BIBLIOGRAPHY

lxxviii   http://www.takepart.com/article/2012/12/20/us-rates-mental-illness-rates-are-persistently-high

lxxix   http://www.webmd.com/mental-health/news/20040601/rate-of-mental-illness-is-staggering

lxxx   *http://www.aacap.org/AACAP/Families_and_Youth/ Facts_for_Families/Facts_for_Families_Pages/Children_And_Wat_54.aspx*

lxxxi   Huston, A. C., & Wright, J. C. (1996). University of Kansas, Television and Socialization of Young Children; MacBeth, p. 38

lxxxii   American Psychiatric Association

lxxxiii   Eron, Leonard, Senior Research Scientist at the University of Michigan

lxxxiv   Healy, Jane M. Ph.D. (May 1998). American Academy of Pediatrics- Understanding TV's Effects on the Developing Brain; AAP News

lxxxv   http://www.huffingtonpost.com/cris-rowan/10-reasons-why-handheld-devices-should-be-banned_b_4899218.html

lxxxvi   http://www.huffingtonpost.com/cris-rowan/10-reasons-why-handheld-devices-should-be-banned_b_4899218.html - (Bristol University 2010, Mentzoni 2011, Shin 2011, Liberatore 2011, Robinson 2008)

lxxxvii   http://www.huffingtonpost.com/cris-rowan/10-reasons-why-handheld-devices-should-be-banned_b_4899218.html - (Waddell 2007)

lxxxviii   Rowan 2010 and Gentile 2009 - http://www.huffingtonpost.com/cris-rowan/10-reasons-why-handheld-devices-should-be-banned_b_4899218.html

lxxxix   http://health.usnews.com/health-news/news/articles/2012/08/21/unhappy-kids-are-more-materialistic-study-finds

xc   http://news.bbc.co.uk/2/hi/uk_news/6359849.stm

xci   The National Eating Disorders Association and Screening for Mental Health; http://www.hsph.harvard.edu/striped/files/2012/10/nedsp_evaluation_report.pdf

xcii   Wolf, Naomi (September 24, 2002). The Beauty Myth: How Images of Beauty Are Used Against Women; Harper Perennial

xciii   Wolf, Naomi (September 24, 2002). The Beauty Myth: How Images of Beauty Are Used Against Women; Harper Perennial

xciv   Wolf, Naomi (September 24, 2002). The Beauty Myth: How Images of Beauty Are Used Against Women; Harper Perennial

xcv   http://www.forbes.com/sites/christopherhelman/2013/01/09/the-worlds-happiest-and-saddest-countries-2/2/

xcvi   http://www.workhealth.org/whatsnew/lpkarosh.html*http://www.workhealth.org/whatsnew/lpkarosh.html*

xcvii	Japanese Salarymen Fight Back, The New York Times, Wednesday, June 11, 2008
xcviii	http://www.ncbi.nlm.nih.gov/pubmed/17256448
xcix	http://www.eturbonews.com/37917/denmark-named-world-s-happiest-country-again
c	http://www.eturbonews.com/37917/denmark-named-world-s-happiest-country-again
ci	http://www.ibtimes.com/worlds-happiest-countries-2013-according-un-1403880
cii	https://realitysandwich.com/178885/shannon_error/
ciii	http://www.realitysandwich.com/shannon_error
civ	Suzuki, Shunryu (2002). Not Always So: Practicing the True Spirit of Zen; New York, NY: Harper Collins, p. 35
cv	http://www.psychologytoday.com/print/101595 July 22, 2012
cvi	www.greenspirit.org.uk/resources/UniverseStory
cvii	Nelson, Melissa K. (2008). Original Instructions: Indigenous Teachings for a Sustainable Future; Bear & Company
cviii	The Overview Effect: Space Exploration and Human Evolution, 2nd Edition; Library of Flight, pp. 36–37
cix	Narby, Jeremy (2006). Intelligence in Nature: An Inquiry into Knowledge; Tarcher
cx	Elgin, Duane (2009). The Living Universe: Where Are We? Who Are We? Where Are We Going?; Berrett-Koehler Publishers, p. 45
cxi	Elgin, Duane (2009). The Living Universe: Where Are We? Who Are We? Where Are We Going?; Berrett-Koehler Publishers, p. 46
cxii	Elgin, Duane (2009). The Living Universe: Where are We? Who Are We? Where Are We Going?; Berrett-Koehler Publishers, p. 46
cxiii	Nelson, Melissa K. (2008). Original Instructions: Indigenous Teachings for a Sustainable Future; Bear & Company
cxiv	Fox, Matthew (1983). Meditations with Meister Eckhart; Bear & Company, p. 24
cxv	Elgin, Duane (2009). The Living Universe: Where Are We? Who Are We? Where Are We Going?; Berrett-Koehler Publishers, p. 65
cxvi	The Neo-Platonists, Plotinus quoted in John Gregory (1991). Selected Passages from the Enneads, 4.4.32
cxvii	http://en.wikipedia.org/wiki/Flower_of_Life

BIBLIOGRAPHY

cxviii   www.wiserearth.org

cxix   Chopra, Deepak (2004). The Spontaneous Fulfillment of Desire: Harnessing the Infinite Power of Coincidence; Harmony

cxx   Chopra, Deepak (2004). The Spontaneous Fulfillment of Desire: Harnessing the Infinite Power of Coincidence; Harmony

cxxi   Chopra, Deepak (2004). The Spontaneous Fulfillment of Desire: Harnessing the Infinite Power of Coincidence; Harmony

cxxii   Steffen, Alex (2008). WorldChanging: A User's Guide for the 21st Century; Abrams

cxxiii   http://www.orionmagazine.org/index.php/articles/article/265/

cxxiv   http://www.orionmagazine.org/index.php/articles/article/265/

cxxv   Sinek, Simon (2011). Start with Why: How Great Leaders Inspire Everyone to Take Action; Portfolio Trade

cxxvi   Altucher, James (2013). Choose Yourself!; CreateSpace Independent Publishing Platform

cxxvii   http://money.cnn.com/2013/09/15/news/economy/income-inequality-obama/index.html

cxxviii   http://www.entrepreneur.com/article/228176

cxxix   http://www.entrepreneur.com/article/228176

cxxx   http://www.fastcoexist.com/1679903/the-rise-of-the-micro-entrepreneurship-economy

cxxxi   http://www.newgeography.com/content/003761-toward-a-self-employed-nation

cxxxii   http://www.today.com/moms/brink-many-working-moms-falling-apart-author-says-4B11184706

cxxxiii   http://www.today.com/moms/brink-many-working-moms-falling-apart-author-says-4B11184706

cxxxiv   *http://www.careerbuilder.com/share/aboutus/pressreleasesdetail.aspx?id=pr695&sd=5/9/2012&ed=12/31/2012*

cxxxv   http://www.americanprogress.org/issues/labor/report/2013/04/26/61538/lessons-learned/

cxxxvi   http://fox6now.com/2012/03/05/milwaukee-medical-staffing-company-to-pay-148000/

cxxxvii   http://jobs.aol.com/articles/2012/04/05/epidemic-of-pregnant-women-getting-fired-legal-loopholes-to-bla/

cxxxviii   http://jobs.aol.com/articles/2013/02/05/fmla-maternity-leave-families-medical-leave/

cxxxix	http://www.forbes.com/special-report/2012/30-under-30/30-under-30_social.html
cxl	http://www.forbes.com/special-report/2012/30-under-30/30-under-30_social.html
cxli	http://www.hawaiianlife.com/content/meaning-rainbow
cxlii	Nelson, Melissa K (2008). Original Instructions: Indigenous Teachings for a Sustainable Future; Bear & Company
cxliii	Eknath, Easwaran (1993). The Compassionate Universe: The Power of the Individual to Heal the Environment; Nilgiri Press
cxliv	http://www.pbs.org/wgbh/nova/physics/spooky-action-distance.html
cxlv	http://www.pbs.org/wgbh/nova/physics/spooky-action-distance.html
cxlvi	http://www.pbs.org/wgbh/nova/physics/spooky-action-distance.html
cxlvii	http://noosphere.princeton.edu
cxlviii	http://www.pachamama.org/blog/we-are-one-the-science-of-interconnectedness
cxlix	Morrell, Rima. The Sacred Power of Huna, Spirituality and Shamanism in Hawai'i, Ph.D., pp. 82–83
cl	http://www.hunawisdom.com/ancient_secrets
cli	http://www.hunawisdom.com/ancient_secrets
clii	King, Serge Kahili (1990). Urban Shaman; Simon & Schuster, pp. 52–81. ISBN 0-671-68307-1.
cliii	http://www.laughteryogaamerica.com/4fun/grow/practice-hooponopono-simple-steps-1183.php
cliv	http://spiritualcompassconnection.com/hooponopono.html
clv	Morrell, Rima. The Sacred Power of Huna, Spirituality and Shamanism in Hawai'i, Ph.D., p. 194
clvi	http://www.huffingtonpost.com/ocean-robbins/having-gratitude-_b_1073105.html
clvii	Emmons, Robert, and Michael McCullough. "Counting Blessings Versus Burdens: An Experimental Investigation of Gratitude and Subjective Well-Being in Daily Life." *Journal of Personality and Social Psychology* 84.2 (2003): 377–389. Print.
clviii	Easwaran, Eknath (May 17, 2007). The Bhagavad Gita; Nilgiri Press; 2nd edition
clix	Easwaran, Eknath (May 17, 2007). The Bhagavad Gita; Nilgiri Press; 2nd edition, p. 12

BIBLIOGRAPHY

clx   Schmidt, Victoria Lynn (August 15, 2007). 45 Master Characters; Writers Digest

clxi   Schmidt, Victoria Lynn (August 15, 2007). 45 Master Characters; Writers Digest

clxii   http://flutiebear.tumblr.com/post/22840957119/taking-the-heroines-journey-how-this-often-overlooked

clxiii   Attar, Farid (2005). The Conference of the Birds; Penguin, pp. 854–74

clxiv   Easwaran, Eknath (August 28, 2007). The Upanishads; Nilgiri Press; 2nd edition, Brihadaranyaka IV.

clxv   Easwaran, Eknath (May 17, 2007). The Bhagavad Gita; Nilgiri Press; 2nd edition, 9:27

clxvi   http://www.amazon.com/Super-Brain-Unleashing-Explosive-Well-Being/dp/0307956822/ref=cm_cr_pr_product_top

clxvii   Easwaran, Eknath (May 17, 2007). The Bhagavad Gita; Nilgiri Press; 2nd edition

clxviii   Dispenza, Joe (2013). Breaking The Habit of Being Yourself: How to Lose Your Mind and Create a New One; Hay House

clxix   Dispenza, Joe (2013). Breaking The Habit of Being Yourself: How to Lose Your Mind and Create a New One; Hay House

clxx   Shankaranarayanan, S. (1979). Sri Chakra; Dipti Publications; 3rd edition

clxxi   Everly, George S. and Jeffrey M. Lating (2002). A Clinical Guide to the Treatment of Human Stress Response. ISBN 0-306-46620-1 p. 199

clxxii   Easwaran, Eknath (May 17, 2007). The Bhagavad Gita; Nilgiri Press; 2nd edition, p. 17

clxxiii   Safran, Jeremy (2003). Psychoanalysis and Buddhism: An Unfolding Dialogue, Wisdom Publications, p. 173

clxxiv   Osho International Foundation (2011). The Empty Boat: Encounters with Nothingness; Osho, Chapter 10

clxxv   http://theyogablog.com/an-md-explains-your-brain-on-meditation/

clxxvi   http://www.toolsforwellness.com/brainstates.html

clxxvii   http://www.allthingshealing.com/healing-through-storytelling.php#.UkXdXBaRh8s

clxxviii   http://annals.org/article.aspx?articleid=746718

clxxix   http://www.nytimes.com/2011/02/10/health/views/10chen.html

clxxx   Steffen, Alex (2008). WorldChanging: A User's Guide for the 21st Century; Abrams clxxxi Steffen, Alex (2008). WorldChanging: A User's Guide for the 21st Century; Abrams

clxxxii Friedrich von Schiller, Johann Christoph. The Piccolomini, Kindle Edition

clxxxiii http://cojmc.unl.edu/nativedaughters/storytellers/native-storytellers-connect-the-past-and-the-future

clxxxiv Steffen, Alex (2008). WorldChanging: A User's Guide for the 21st Century; Abrams

www.ingramcontent.com/pod-product-compliance
Lightning Source LLC
Chambersburg PA
CBHW020003050426
42450CB00005B/292